SHE DESERVES
MORE THAN POTENTIAL

Ernsie Fidelia

She Deserves More Than Potential

By Ernsie Fidelia

Ernsie Fidelia

Because of the dynamic nature of the Internet, any web addresses or links contained in this book may have changed since publication and may no longer be valid.

Paperback ISBN-13: 979-8-9998412-8-5
HardCover ISBN-13: 979-8-9953874-0-4
eBook (Kindle): 979-8-9953874-1-1

First edition published in 2026. Published in the United States.

Published by:

What is Holistic Health, LLC, Tampa, Florida

What This Book Will Do For You

- Stop second-guessing your intuition
- Recognize red flags early
- Break emotional patterns
- Set standards without guilt
- Choose peace over confusion
- Walk away without needing closure

"This is about finally choosing yourself."

Table of Contents

Dedication xi

Prologue xiii

Introduction xvii

THE P.O.P METHOD™ xxi

PART 1: THE CONFUSION 1

Chapter One: Inconsistency — When His Words Do Not Match His Actions 3

Chapter Two: Mixed Signals Are Still a Signal — Confusion is Not Care 13

Chapter Three: Hot and Cold Behavior — Inconsistency Is a Red Flag 19

Chapter Four: Breadcrumbing — She Deserves More Than Potential 25

PART 2: THE ILLUSION 33

Chapter Five: Future Faking — "Someday" Love That Never Arrives 35

Chapter Six: Potential Versus Reality — When Words Do Not Match Actions Believe the Action...............43

Chapter Seven: Half-Love Killing You? — Let Go Before You Break 49

Chapter Eight: Delayed Commitment — When He Keeps You in Limbo 55

PART 3: THE PATTERN 63

Chapter Nine: Emotional Unavailability — He's Here, But He's Not Present.. 65

Chapter Ten: Bare Minimum Effort — Loving You Only When You Complain 73

Chapter Eleven: Excuses / Justification — Empty Apologies Does Not Mean Change 81

Chapter Twelve: Confusion as a Pattern — Are You Asking the Wrong Man?.................................. 87

PART 4: THE INTERNAL SHIFT 93

Chapter Thirteen: Overgiving — When "Protection" Feels Like Possession 95

Chapter Fourteen: Ignoring the Red Flags — Gaslighting 101

Chapter Fifteen: Dependency of Emotional Labor — You Are Doing All the Work..............................109

Chapter Sixteen: Self-Abandonment — Cheating Is Not a Mistake It is a Choice..............................115

PART 5: THE BREAK 121

Chapter Seventeen: Losing Yourself, Reclaiming Your Power — Coming Home to Yourself 123

Chapter Eighteen: The Turning Point — Choosing Solitude Over Chaos 131

Chapter Nineteen: Detaching — Love Should Not Hurt 137

Chapter Twenty: Final Realization — Choosing Yourself is the Highest Form of Love 145

Epilogue 151
The Standard She Now Walks In 155
The Crowned Woman Standard Oath 157
Other Books by Ernsie Fidelia 159
About the Author 161

Dedication

To my children

Taquan, Aniya, and Alice:

You are the reason I rise, the reason I build, and the reason I refuse to settle. Everything I create is rooted in my love for you.

And to every woman surviving on "potential":

You were never meant to live half-seen or half-valued. May these pages awaken you to the truth you are already worthy of more.

Prologue

Many women are not heartbroken — they are exhausted.

Exhausted from confusion, inconsistency, and emotional labor.

There is a kind of heartbreak that doesn't come from betrayal. It comes from realization. Realizing he was never going to become the version of him you built in your head.

Realizing the effort you were waiting for was never coming.

Realizing the "almost" you kept holding onto was the most he was ever going to give.

No one talks about the grief of potential.

The grief of who he could have been.

The grief of the future you imagined.

The grief of the ring you pictured.

The house. The stability. The partnership.

You weren't in love with who he was.

You were in love with who he could be if he tried.

And that is a dangerous kind of love.

Because it keeps you loyal to a version of a man that doesn't exist.

So, you wait.

You excuse.

You rationalize.

You call red flags misunderstandings.

You call inconsistency stress.

You call emotional unavailability trauma.

You call bare minimum effort "he's trying."

But deep down—you know.

You know love isn't supposed to feel like this.

You know peace doesn't feel like anxiety.

You know being chosen doesn't feel like guessing.

This book was written for the moment when denial finally collapses — when clarity hurts, and the fantasy dies.

When you finally admit: "I have been settling."

And instead of breaking you—that truth sets you free.

Introduction

Let's tell the truth.

You didn't stay because you were weak.

You stayed because you loved deeply.

You stayed because you saw potential in people.

You stayed because you believed in growth.

You stayed because you don't quit easily.

But somewhere along the way, your strength turned into self-sacrifice.

Your patience turned into self-abandonment.

Your loyalty turned into self-betrayal.

You started calling survival love.

You started calling crumbs effort.

You started calling chaos passion.

You started calling mixed signals chemistry.

You started calling emotional starvation "just a phase."

And the scariest part? You adjusted.

You adjusted your standards.

Your expectations.

Your voice.

Your boundaries.

Yourself.

Until one day you didn't even recognize who you were anymore.

This book is not here to blame him. It is here to wake you up.

Because the moment you stop blaming yourself for wanting consistency... everything changes.

You were never too much.

You were just giving your heart to someone who only had half of one to offer.

You don't need another almost. You don't need another someday. You don't need potential.

You need proof.

THE P.O.P METHOD™

"This is your new standard for every relationship."

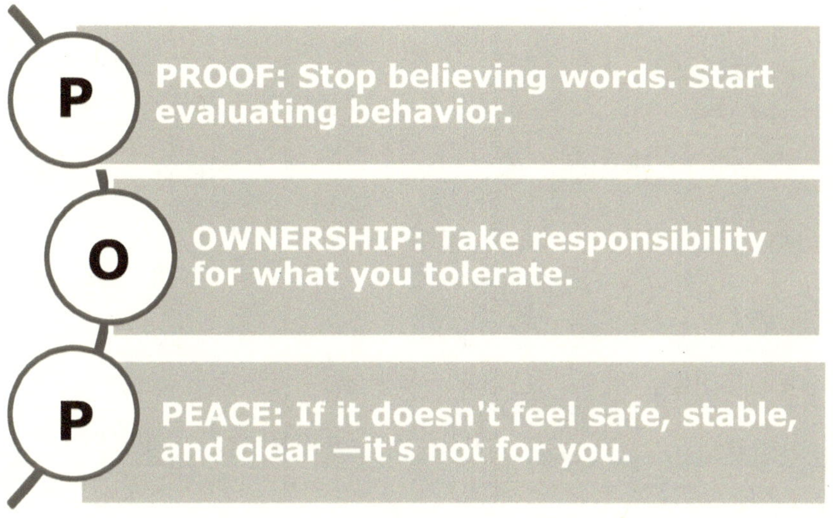

This book is designed to go along with

DESERVE MORE THAN POTENTIAL™
The P.O.P Method™ Workbook

A Guided System for Breaking Cycles, Rebuilding Standards, and Choosing Yourself

By Ernsie Fidelia

PART 1:

THE CONFUSION

Boy, Can I Relate!

It Feels So Familiar and Relatable.

Chapter One

Inconsistency — When His Words Do Not Match His Actions

We have all been there. Sitting with our phone in hand, replaying conversations in our heads, trying to make sense of the gap between what he said and what he did.

He said he would call. He did not.

He said he would show up. He did not.

He said he loved you — but his actions kept saying otherwise.

At first, you excused it. Everybody gets busy. Everybody slips up sometimes. You told yourself not to be "too sensitive," not to nag, not to expect too much. You held on to the words because they were beautiful, even though the actions left you empty.

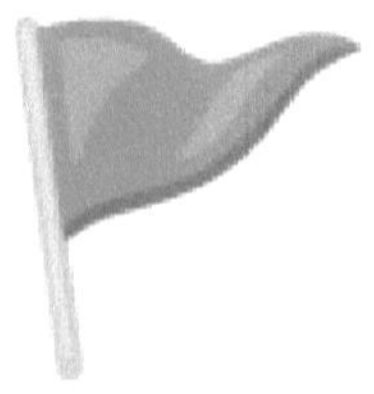

Red Flag: That is how inconsistency works — it feeds you just enough to keep you from starving, but never enough to fill you.

The Illusion of "Sometimes"

When he is good, he is good.

Those mornings when he texts before you are even awake. Those nights when he shows up with your favorite food.

Those weekends where he is all in — planning, laughing, loving you the way you have always wanted.

And in those moments, you breathe. You convince yourself; this is who he really is. This is why you stay. This is why I stayed.

But then it shifts. The texts slow down. The calls stop. The plans fade. You go from priority to afterthought without warning. And you are left replaying the highs and the lows.

That is the cruelty of inconsistency: the highs are just enough to blind you to the truth of the lows. You cling to the memory of his best days while excusing his worst ones.

Here is the reality: if love is unstable, it is unsafe.

The BS They Tell Us

■ You know the lines:

- "I've just been busy."
- "You know I care about you; I just have a lot going on."
- "I'm trying, can't you see that?"
- "You always focus on the negative."

They sound reasonable, don't they? Enough to make you pause, to doubt yourself, to feel guilty for even bringing it up.

But here is the truth behind the words:

Translation:

Words	Actions
"I've just been busy."	"I didn't prioritize you."
"You know I care."	"I hope my words distract you from my lack of effort."
"I'm trying."	"I want credit for the bare minimum."
"You always focus on the negative."	"I don't want to take responsibility."

Red Flag: If his effort only shows up when you complain, it is not love. It is damage control.

Why We Stay

You checked your phone more than you wanted to admit.

Because when he showed up, everything felt different.

And when he didn't—

you felt it just as strongly.

We stay because inconsistency feels like hope.

We tell ourselves if he could love me like that once, he can do it again.

We stay because inconsistency feels like gambling. The highs are addictive. When he finally does what we have been begging for, the relief feels like a jackpot. And so, we pull the lever repeatedly, hoping for another win.

We stay because we have been conditioned to. We have been taught that men are "just like that," that women must be patient, that "nobody's perfect."

But let us tell the truth: Inconsistency is not imperfection. It is a decision. And every time we excuse it, we betray ourselves.

The Cost of Staying

Inconsistency does not just waste time — it eats at your soul.

- You start questioning yourself instead of questioning him.
- You lower your standards to avoid sounding "demanding."
- You teach yourself to settle for crumbs while calling it a meal.

And the longer you stay, the more you forget what real love feels like. You mistake chaos for passion. You confuse anxiety with butterflies. You normalize being half-loved until you cannot remember what being fully chosen even looks like.

But the cost is bigger than heartbreak.

It is sleepless nights.

It is stress in your body.

It is losing pieces of yourself that were never meant to be given away so cheaply.

Healing from Inconsistency

The first step is honesty. Call it what it is: not stress, not distraction, not imperfection.

Disrespect.

Then, create a standard you refuse to bend on:

- If he disappears without communication, you will not chase.
- If he promises and does not deliver, you will not excuse.
- If his actions do not match his words, you will believe the actions.

You do not need to explain your worth to someone who already knows it and chooses not to honor it.

Red Flag Checklist

- Does he show up only when you threaten to leave?

- Does he apologize often but rarely change?
- Does he give you enough love to keep you, but not enough to make you feel secure?
- Do you feel more anxious than at peace in this relationship?

If you answered yes, inconsistency is running the show.

Reflection Prompts

1. Think of the last time his actions did not match his words. How did you explain it away?
2. What patterns of inconsistency have you excused more than once?
3. What would it look like if you stopped waiting for him to get it right?

Healing Steps

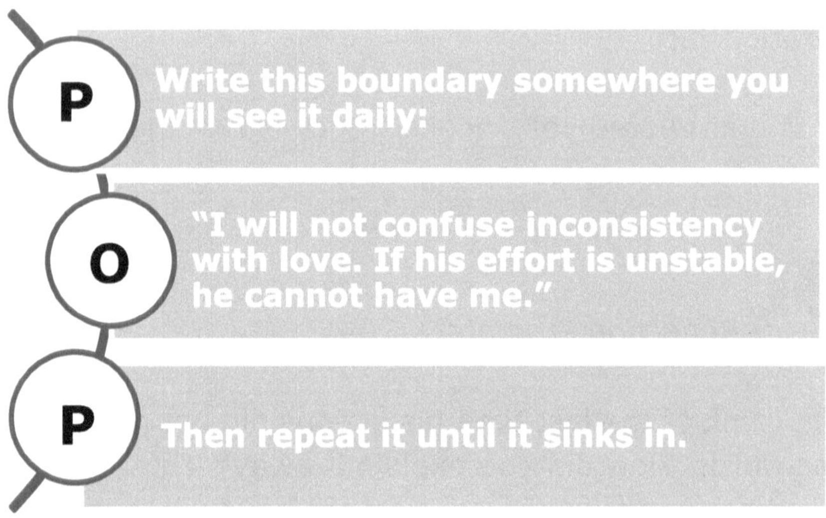

Closing Truth

Inconsistency is not love.

Love shows up. Love does not vanish and reappear when it feels like it. Love does not leave you questioning if you matter.

If he is not consistent, he is not committed. If he is not steady, he is not safe.

If he is not all in, he is not your person.

And the sooner you believe that the sooner you will stop wasting years waiting for potential.

Because we do not just deserve love.

We deserve consistency.

We deserve peace.

We deserve more than potential.

The Truth:

Consistency is not effort.
It is character.

Chapter Two

Mixed Signals Are Still a Signal — Confusion is Not Care

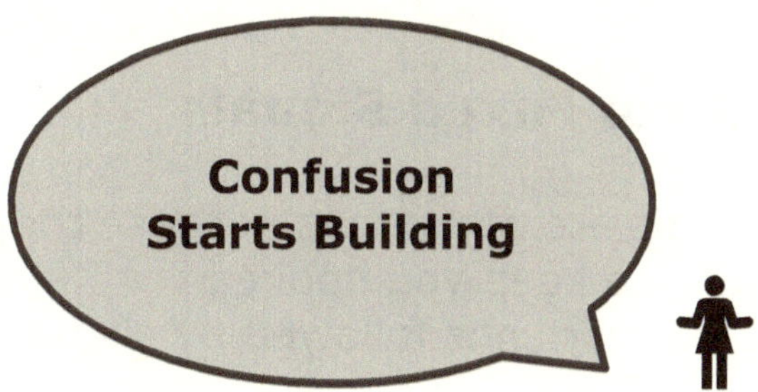

He says he loves you but disappears for days.

He calls you "his everything," but does not prioritize you.

He plans a future with you in words, but in action, you are always left wondering.

And you tell yourself he is just figuring things out. You convince yourself he just needs time. You hold on because the mixed signals keep you hoping — he would not say those things if he did not mean them, right?

Red Flag: Mixed signals are still a signal. And that signal is: he's not ready, he's not consistent, he is not your peace.

The Trap of Mixed Signals

Mixed signals are dangerous because they give you just enough to keep you hooked.

- The good mornings followed by silence for the rest of the day.
- The deep conversations that vanish into cold distance the next week.
- The "you're my forever" words paired with half-hearted actions. This push-pull cycle keeps you questioning yourself instead of questioning him. It is not love — its instability dressed as passion.

 *Red Flag:* If love leaves you confused, it is not love.

The BS They Tell Us

■ Common Lines:

- "I'm just bad at communication."
- "You know how I feel, I don't always have to show it."
- "You're reading too much into it."
- "Things are complicated right now."

Translation:

Words	Actions
"I'm bad at communication."	"I do not value making you feel secure."
"You know how I feel."	"I want credit for the effort that I am not giving."
"You're reading too much."	"I want you to stop noticing my inconsistency."
"It's complicated."	"I do not want to commit, but I do not want to lose you either."

Why We Stay

> He spoke about the future like it was already yours.
>
> And for a moment,
>
> you forgot to look at what he was doing right now.

Because the good moments feel real. Because when he shows up, he shows up so well that you convince yourself that is the real him. Because you want to believe you are not wasting your time, so you cling to the highs and excuse the lows.

But real love does not come in highs and lows. Real love is steady.

Real love is certain.

Real love does not leave you checking your phone in confusion every night.

The Cost of Mixed Signals

- You start overanalyzing everything he says or does not say.
- You live in anxiety instead of peace.
- You mistake drama for passion.
- You begin to think inconsistency is normal.

But the cost is deeper: Confusion drains your spirit. It steals your joy. It replaces your clarity with constant second-guessing.

Red Flag Checklist

- He only gives effort when he feels you pulling away.
- He says one thing and does another.

- You are constantly asking yourself where you stand.
- You have spent more time decoding his actions than enjoying the relationship.

Reflection Prompts

1. When was the last time you felt genuinely secure in this relationship?
2. How often do his actions and words truly align?
3. If your best friend described the same situation to you, would you call it love or confusion?

Healing Steps

P — **Believe the Inconsistency. Stop chasing the good moments as proof of his love. See the whole pattern.**

O — **Define Clarity. Write down what consistent love looks like for you and measure his actions against it.**

P — **Affirm Daily: "Love is not supposed to confuse me. If it brings me chaos, it is not for me."**

Closing Truth

Confusion is not care. Care is clear. Love is consistent. Real commitment does not come with disclaimers.

If you are left feeling lost, uncertain, or insecure, that is not a soulmate — that is a distraction.

We are not decoding mixed signals anymore. We are not staying in chaos anymore.

We are not confusing words with proof anymore. Because we do not just deserve words.

We deserve clarity. We deserve certainty. We deserve more than potential.

The Truth:

Mixed signals are still signals.

Chapter Three

Hot and Cold Behavior — Inconsistency Is a Red Flag

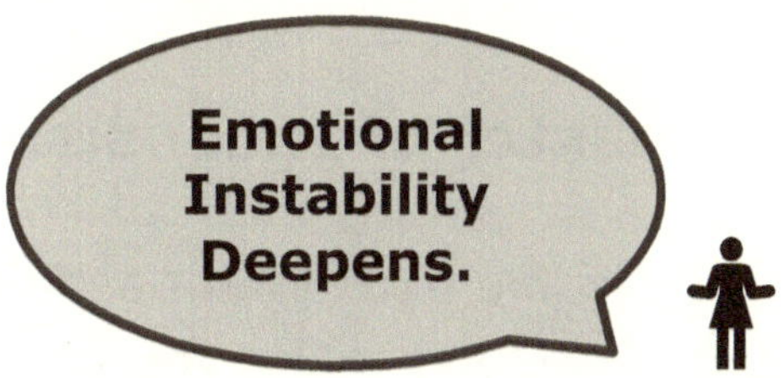

One day he is all in. The texts, the calls, the effort — he shows up. You feel wanted. You feel chosen. You feel like, finally, he sees you.

Then suddenly, the switch flips.

The messages slow down. His attention drifts. His effort fades. And you're left replaying everything in your head, wondering what you did wrong.

Red Flag: Inconsistency is not a personality trait. It is a choice. A man who truly values you will not be hot one day and cold the next — he will stay steady, even when it's not convenient.

The Roller-coaster of Inconsistent Love

Inconsistency feels like excitement at first. The highs are intoxicating. The lows make you chase the next high even harder. You confuse the adrenaline of unpredictability with passion.

But love is not supposed to feel like a rollercoaster.

It's supposed to feel like a foundation.
- He calls daily, then disappears for days.
- He is affectionate in public, but distant in private.
- He promises commitment but acts single when it suits him. This is not love. It's chaos dressed as romance.

 The BS They Tell Us

■ Excuses of the Inconsistent Man:
- "I've just been busy."
- "You're overthinking it."
- "You know how I feel about you; I don't need to say it every day."

- "I'll do better, just give me time."

Translation:

Words	Actions
"Busy."	"I prioritize everything else before you."
"Overthinking."	"I want you to silence your intuition."
"You know how I feel."	"I want credit without consistency."
"I'll do better."	"I will do just enough to keep you, then fade again."

Why We Stay

> One conversation made everything feel clear.
>
> The next made you question everything.
>
> And somehow, you kept trying to make both versions make sense.

Because the good days are so good.

Because when he is present, it feels real.

Because we believe the inconsistency means he is struggling, not that he is choosing.

But the truth? Inconsistency is a decision. Love that is real does not require reminders, threats, or begging.

The Cost of Inconsistency

- You start doubting yourself instead of doubting his effort.
- You live in anxiety, waiting for the next drop in energy.
- You confuse chaos for chemistry.
- You start calling inconsistency "normal."

But the cost is deeper: Inconsistency robs you of security. And love without security is just pain wrapped in romance.

Red Flag Checklist

- His effort comes in waves instead of staying steady.
- You are more focused on keeping his attention than enjoying his presence.
- You feel like you are constantly guessing where you stand.
- His promises are temporary fixes instead of permanent change.

Reflection Prompts

1. What is the longest his "effort streak" has ever lasted?
2. How do you feel when his energy drops — and why do you excuse it?
3. What would it look like to demand consistency as the baseline, not the exception?

Healing Steps

P — **See the Pattern. Stop treating inconsistency as random. It is deliberate.**

O — **Raise the Standard. Decide what consistent effort looks like and refuse to accept less.**

P — **Affirm Daily: "Consistency is love in action. I will not accept love that disappears when it's inconvenient."**

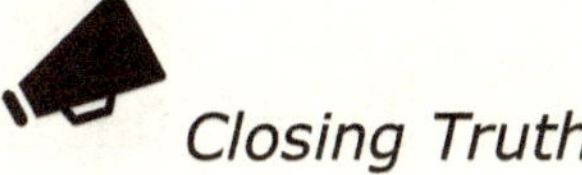

Closing Truth

Inconsistent love keeps you trapped in cycles of hope

and disappointment. It makes you feel like you are always one step away from being truly chosen.

But real love does not make you guess. It does not fade when life gets busy. It doesn't confuse you with hot-and-cold behavior.

If a man cannot show up consistently, he is not ready. He is not capable. He is not your peace.

We are not chasing highs anymore.

We are not surviving on "sometimes" anymore.

We are not confusing chaos with chemistry anymore.

Because we do not just deserve effort when it is convenient.

We deserve consistency. We deserve security. We deserve more than potential.

The Truth:

Inconsistency is not a personality trait. It is a choice.

Chapter Four

Breadcrumbing — She Deserves More Than Potential

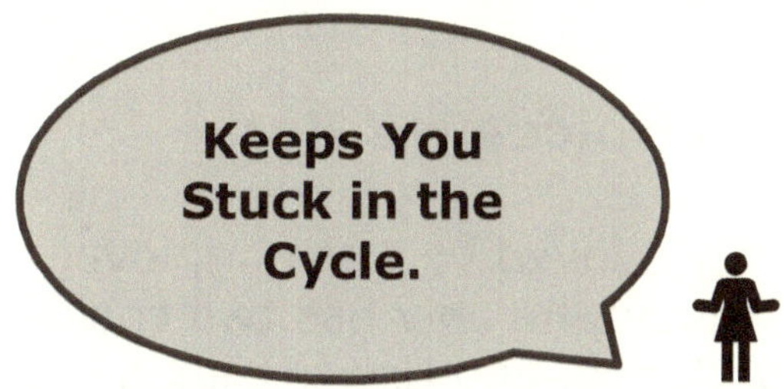

A woman like you cannot be half-loved.

You cannot be given crumbs and expected to starve quietly.

You cannot be someone's "almost," someone's "maybe," someone's placeholder while he figures himself out.

You have given your loyalty. You have given your softness. You have given your strength. And in return, too many men have given you potential — the idea of who they might be, instead of the truth of who they are.

Red Flag: Potential is not love. Potential is a promise without proof, a fantasy without follow-through, a word without weight.

The Two Choices He Has

When a man is loved by a strong, loyal, emotionally invested woman, he only has two choices:

1. Step up, grow, and rise to match her effort.
2. Step aside and make space for a man who can.

It is that simple. There is no middle ground. You cannot "half-love" a woman like her. You cannot breadcrumb her with words while withholding action. You cannot keep her waiting for years while you dabble in immaturity. Because she is not a placeholder. She is a purpose.

 The BS They Tell Us

■ Excuses of Men Who Cannot Handle Her:

- "You deserve better than me."
- "I'm not ready, but don't give up on me."
- "You're intimidating."
- "I need to figure myself out first."

Translation:

Words	Actions
"You deserve better."	"I know it, but I will not give it to you."
"I'm not ready."	"I want your loyalty without giving you commitment."
"You're intimidating."	"Your strength exposes my weakness."
"I need to figure myself out."	"I do not want to grow while you're watching."

Why We Stay

> You told yourself you were done.
>
> And then he reached out.
>
> Not enough to fix it—
>
> just enough to restart it.

Because we see the best in people. Because we want to believe our love can inspire them to change. Because we think walking away makes us impatient, ungrateful, disloyal.

But the truth is: Staying for potential is self-betrayal. You deserve love that is steady now, not "someday."

You deserve consistency today, not "when he gets it together."

You deserve effort without conditions, not only when you threaten to leave.

The Cost of Settling for Potential

- You waste years waiting on "almost."
- You live in confusion instead of clarity.
- You dim your own light, so he does not feel insecure.
- You teach yourself to celebrate promises instead of progress.

The cost of potential is your peace. And your peace is too expensive to gamble on someone else's immaturity.

Red Flag Checklist

- He talks about what he will do but never does it.
- He needs constant "reminders" to act right.
- You feel like his teacher instead of his partner.
- You spend more time defending his potential than experiencing his presence.

Reflection Prompts

1. What "potential" have you been waiting for him to fulfill?
2. How long have you been holding on to words without action?
3. What would life look like if you only accepted men who matched your energy now?

Healing Steps

P — **Stop Romanticizing Potential. Love the man in front of you, not the fantasy of who he could be.**

O — **Set the Standard. Promise yourself you will not settle for half-love, empty promises, or "someday" love again.**

P — **Affirm Daily: "I deserve love that is steady, certain, and real. I am no longer waiting for potential — I am choosing alignment."**

Closing Truth

She — you — deserve more than potential. You

deserve the man who does not hesitate. The one who does not find your strength intimidating but inspiring. The one who does not make you question your worth but affirms it daily. The one who does not just say he will love you better someday but proves it now.

Because a woman like you cannot be loved halfway. You cannot be silenced, dimmed, or delayed anymore.

You are not "too much." You are not asking for the impossible. You are not unworthy of love when it shows up.

You are the whole meal, the full vision, the prize that was never meant to be gambled with.

And from this chapter forward — you are no longer accepting crumbs, excuses, or empty potential. Because you do not just deserve to be loved.

You deserve to be loved well. Fully. Consistently. Out loud

The Truth:

Potential is not love.
Potential is delay.
Potential is confusion
dressed as hope.

PART 2:

THE ILLUSION

Why We Stay.

Beginning to Understand Why It's So Hard to Set Boundaries.

Chapter Five

Future Faking — "Someday" Love That Never Arrives

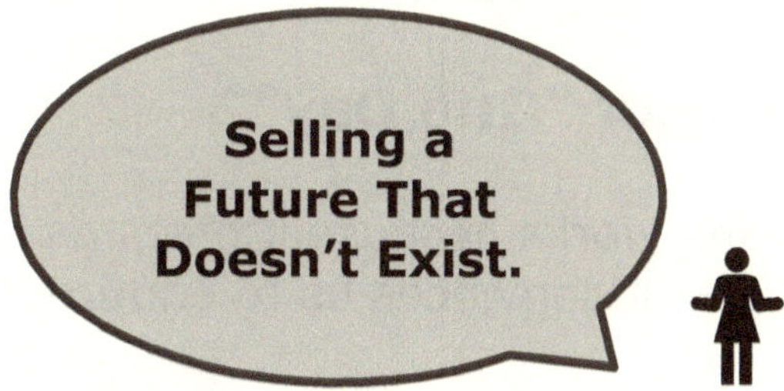

We have all heard the lines before.

"One day I'm going to marry you."

"Once I get myself together, we'll move in."

"I just need some time, but we're forever."

They sound beautiful, don't they? They make you feel chosen, secure, special. They keep you hanging on — because if he is saying it, then surely it must mean he sees a future with you.

Red Flag: Future faking is not a promise. It is a strategy. It is a tactic men use to keep you invested in the relationship without doing the work to make it real.

The Allure of "One Day"

Future faking works because it gives us hope. Hope is powerful — it convinces us to endure things we never should.

He does not show up today, but you tell yourself, "It's okay, because one day, it'll all make sense." He does not make you a priority now, but you cling to the vision he painted of a house, kids, and stability later.

He does not change, but you keep remembering the way he once talked about growing into the man you deserve.

Here is the reality: If he wanted that future, he would be showing it in the present.

The BS They Tell Us

■ Common Lines of a Future Faker:

• "You know I see us together forever."

- "Once I get through this rough patch, things will be different."
- "You just have to be patient with me."
- "I know I've been distant, but that's only because I'm working toward our future."

On the surface, these lines sound romantic. They sound hopeful.

But underneath, they are stalling tactics.

Translation:

Words	Actions
"I see us together forever."	"I like the comfort of you being around, but I'm not making changes to deserve you."
"You have to be patient."	"I want your loyalty without giving you commitment."
"Things will be different."	"I know you're running out of patience, so let me buy more time with empty promises."

Red Flag: If the future is always beautiful but the present is always disappointing, you are being sold a fantasy, not a reality.

Why We Stay

> Every time things started to feel deeper,
>
> he pulled back.
>
> Like closeness had a limit
>
> he couldn't go past.

We fall for future faking because it speaks to our deepest desires. We want stability. We want love that lasts. We want to believe we finally found the man who sees us as his forever.

But here is the danger: When you fall in love with potential, you stop paying attention to reality. You trade your present peace for a vision of tomorrow that may never come.

We hold on because we do not want to feel like the time we have already invested was wasted.

We tell ourselves we have come too far to quit. But every day that we stay for "someday," we lose today.

The Cost of Future Faking

Future faking robs us of more than time. It robs us of our trust in ourselves. Every time we believe a promise that never comes true, we start doubting our instincts. We wonder if we are expecting too much. We wonder if the problem is us.

But here is the truth:
You are not too much.
You are not impatient.
You are not asking for the impossible.

You are simply asking for someone who can show up now, not 'someday.'

Red Flag Checklist

- He talks about marriage but never introduces you to his family.
- He promises stability but cannot even handle the basics now.
- He talks about building a future while leaving you insecure in the present.
- His "plans" have no timeline, no action steps, no follow-through.

Reflection Prompts

1. Write down the last "someday" promise you believed. Did he ever act on it?
2. What parts of your present did you sacrifice waiting for his future?

3. If you stopped believing his words and only judged him by his actions, what story would that tell?

Healing Steps

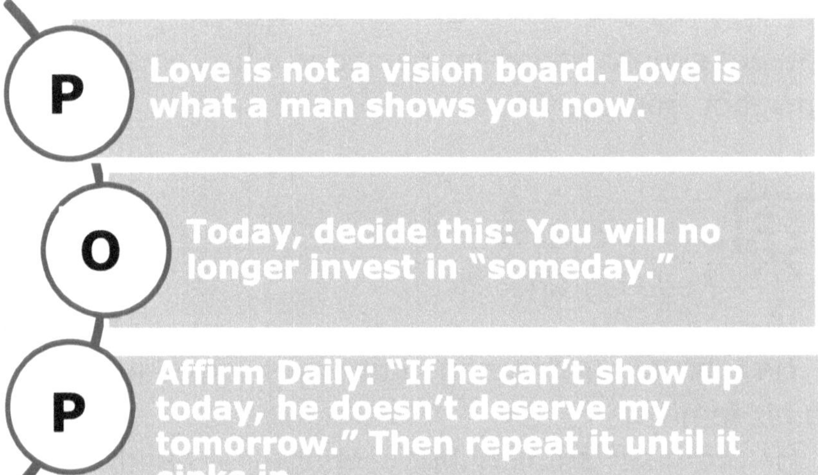

Closing Truth

Future faking is emotional manipulation. It is a way of buying your patience while wasting your time.

A man who genuinely wants you does not just talk about the future — he builds it with you, step by step, right now.

If his love only exists in "one day," it does not exist at all. Because we are done settling for someday.

We deserve presence. We deserve action. We deserve more than potential.

The Truth:

If there is no timeline, there is no intention.

Chapter Six

Potential Versus Reality — When Words Do Not Match Actions Believe the Action

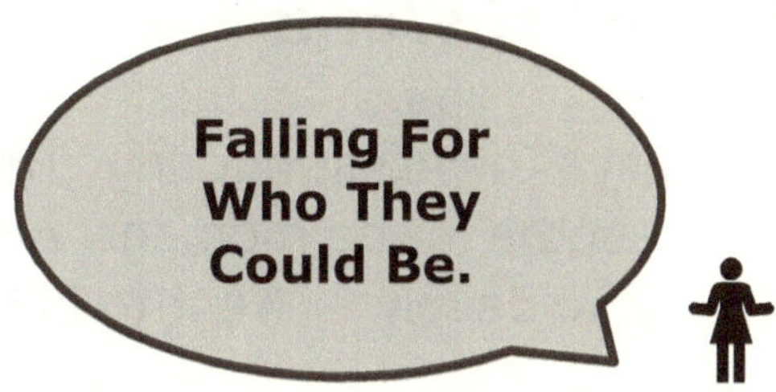

Every Time He says he loves you. But he does not call. He does not show up. He does not keep his promises.

He says you are his priority. But you are always the last to know, the last to be considered, the last to be chosen.

He says you are "the one." But he treats you like a possibility.

Red Flag: When words and actions do not line up, believe the action. Every. Single. Time.

The Comfort of Words

Words are easy. They cost nothing. They sound sweet. They soothe in the moment. And we — as women who love deeply — want to believe them.

So, when he whispers, "I'll do better," we hold on.

When he says, "You're all I want," we forgive.

When he promises "Things will change," we stay.

But here is the truth: words without action are lies dressed as hope.

 The BS They Tell Us

■ Common Empty Promises:

- "I'll call you tomorrow."
- "I'm gonna change, just watch."
- "You're my future, I just need time."
- "You're the only one for me."

Translation:

Words	Actions
"I'll call you tomorrow."	"I am saying what you want to hear in the moment."
"I'm gonna change."	"I want you to stay while I keep doing the same."
"I just need time."	"I want your loyalty while I waste it."
"You're the only one."	"I want exclusivity from you without accountability from me."

Why We Stay

> You noticed you were the one holding everything together.
>
> And when you stopped—
>
> nothing else did.

We believe them because hope is powerful. Because we want to believe love can grow. Because when he says the right thing, it feeds the part of us that remembers why we stayed in the first place.

But words without proof are just fantasies.

And a fantasy cannot build a future.

The Cost of Ignoring the Actions

- You teach yourself to value promises over patterns.
- You waste years waiting on changes that never come.
- You start doubting your own ability to recognize the truth.
- You live in cycles of disappointment disguised as "second chances."

The cost is your clarity. And once you lose clarity, you lose peace.

Red Flag Checklist

- He repeats the same mistakes no matter how many times he apologizes.
- His effort only shows up in words, not in consistent actions.
- You are constantly defending his intentions to others.
- You feel like you are building a future on broken ground.

Reflection Prompts

1. What is the biggest promise he has made but never kept?
2. How long have you been waiting for his actions to match his words?
3. If you only judged him by his actions, what would your relationship look like?

Healing Steps

P — Track the Pattern. Write down every promise he has made versus what he does. The truth will show itself.

O — Stop Romanticizing Words. Promise yourself you will not let "sweet talk" outweigh consistent effort.

P — Affirm Daily: "I will no longer build my love life on promises. I will believe actions every time."

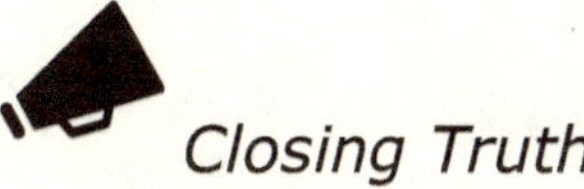

Closing Truth

Words can be beautiful, but actions are the real

language of love. A man who genuinely loves you will not just say it — he will prove it. Every day. In the trivial things. In the hard things. In the consistent, ordinary ways that make love safe.

Do not let sweet talk keep you in confusion. Do not let empty promises waste your years. Do not let words blind you to patterns.

Because we are not falling for lip service anymore.

We are not staying in relationships where words are louder than actions anymore.

We are not mistaking talk for truth anymore.

Because we do not just deserve promises.

We deserve proof. We deserve action. We deserve more than potential.

The Truth:

When words and actions do not line up, believe the action.

Every. Single. Time.

Chapter Seven

Half-Love Killing You? — Let Go Before You Break

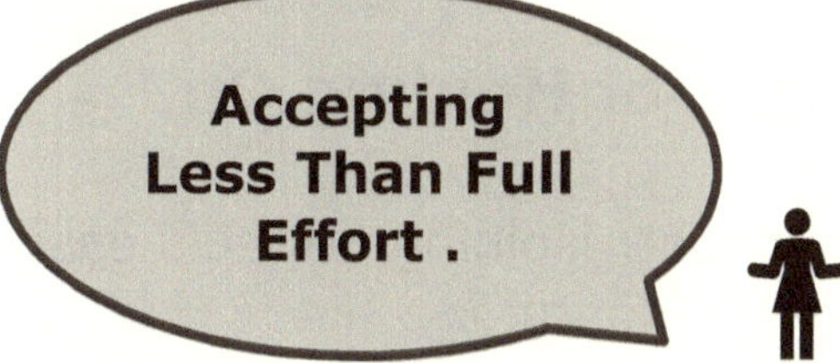

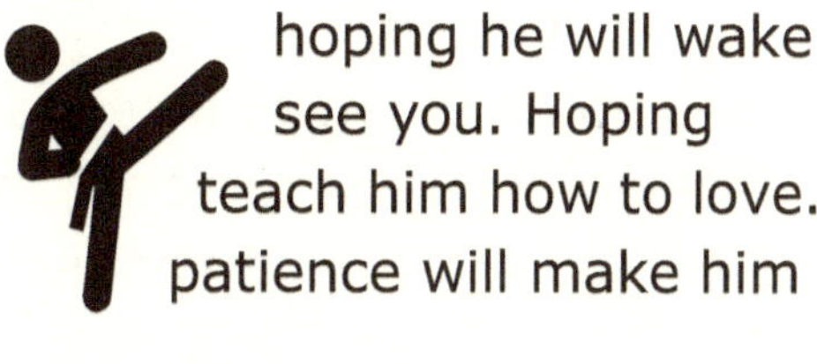

You keep holding on, hoping he will wake up one day and finally see you. Hoping that your loyalty will teach him how to love. Hoping that your patience will make him change.

But while you are waiting for him to "get it together," you are unraveling. While you are holding the relationship together, you are falling apart. While you are pouring love into him, you are running empty.

Red Flag: Staying in a relationship that drains you is not love — it is survival. And survival is different from living.

The Weight of Holding On

Let us be honest: Holding on feels easier than letting go.

- You do not want to "waste" the years you have already invested.
- You do not want to face starting over.
- You do not want to admit that all your sacrifices did not lead to the happy ending you imagined.

So, you hold on tighter. You carry the weight of both your love and his lack. You excuse the pain because "maybe tomorrow will be different."

But every day you stay is another day you betray yourself.

The BS They Tell Us

■ Lines of a Half-Loving Man:

- "I know I need to do better, just give me time."
- "You're the best thing that ever happened to me, don't give up on me."

- "You know I love you, I'm just not good at showing it."
- "If you leave, you'll regret it."

Translation:

Words	Actions
"Give me time."	"I do not plan to change, but I do not want to lose you."
"Don't give up on me."	"I want your loyalty without accountability."
"I love you, but..."	"My words will cover for my lack of effort."
"You'll regret it."	"I want to scare you into staying where I do not value you."

•

Why We Stay

> He said he needed time.
>
> And you gave it.
>
> Until you realized
>
> time wasn't changing anything.

Because we think leaving means failing. Because we would rather fight for the familiar than face the unknown. Because we believe that if we love harder, he will finally rise to meet us.

But let me tell you the truth: You can love someone deeply and still need to leave them. Staying is not proof of strength — sometimes it is proof of fear.

The Cost of Holding on Too Long

- You lose yourself while trying to save him.
- You confuse endurance with love.
- You shrink your needs to fit his convenience.
- You learn to carry heartbreak like it is normal.

The cost of staying too long is not just the relationship. It's your joy, your peace, your identity.

Red Flag Checklist

- You are more exhausted than fulfilled in the relationship.
- He makes promises but never follows through.
- You have stayed more out of history than happiness.
- You cry by yourself more than you laugh together.

Reflection Prompts

1. What is one promise you have been waiting for him to fulfill? How long have you been waiting?
2. What parts of yourself have you lost while holding on?
3. If your daughter or sister were in this same relationship, what advice would you give her?

Healing Steps

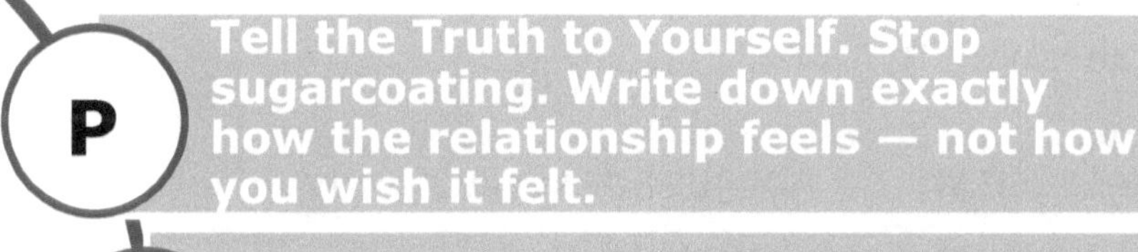

Closing Truth

You have already bent yourself backwards to prove

your love. You have already given him chance after chance. You have already carried the weight of two people in a relationship built for two.

Now it is time to stop breaking for someone who does not deserve the cracks in your soul.

Let go before you lose yourself completely. Let go before your love turns into resentment. Let go before you break — because your healing starts the moment you do. We are not waiting for men to catch up anymore.

We are not wasting years hoping for potential anymore. We are not shrinking ourselves to fit into half-love anymore.

Because we do not just deserve survival.

We deserve joy. We deserve peace. We deserve more than potential.

The Truth:

Staying in a relationship that drains you is not love — it is survival.

Chapter Eight

Delayed Commitment — When He Keeps You in Limbo

He never fully leaves.

But he never fully chooses you either.

You are not single.

But you are not secure.

You are not building.

But you are not walking away.

You are suspended.

Red Flag: When a man keeps you in limbo, he is not confused — he is comfortable.

What Delayed Commitment Looks Like

He calls you his woman but avoids labels.

He talks about the future but refuses timelines.

He wants exclusivity from you but gives you uncertainty in return.

He keeps you emotionally invested while keeping his options emotionally open.

This is not confusion. This is control.

The BS They Tell Us

■ What delayed commitment men say to mask it as love:

- "I just need more time."
- "I'm not ready for that step yet."
- "Let's not rush things."
- "Why put pressure on something good?"

Translation:

Words	Actions
"More time."	"I want you to stick around without commitment."
"I'm not ready."	"Comfort is easier than commitment."
"Let's not rush things."	"Delay provides an exit strategy for me."
"Why put pressure on something good?"	"Limbo lessens the love load."

But months pass. Years pass. And the "right time" never arrives. If he wanted to secure you, he would.

Why We Stay

When he was present, it felt easy.

When he wasn't, it felt confusing.

And you kept trying to figure out how to get back to "easy."

Delayed commitment feels temporary.

But while you are waiting for him to feel ready, you are putting your life on hold.

The longer you wait, the harder it becomes to leave — because now you've invested too much time.

Red Flag Checklist

- He avoids defining the relationship but expects your loyalty.
- He gives just enough attention to keep you from leaving, but never enough to move forward.
- He delays commitment with excuses like timing, healing, or 'not being ready.'
- You feel stuck in uncertainty, constantly waiting for clarity that never comes.

If you see yourself here, you are not in a relationship — you are in a holding pattern.

The Cost of Limbo

You lose clarity.

You lose years.

You lose opportunities for real partnership.

You lose parts of yourself trying to prove you're worth committing to — when you never had to prove it.

Limbo keeps you emotionally occupied while preventing you from being fully loved.

Reflection Prompts

1. How long have you been in "almost"?
2. What step have you been waiting for him to take?
3. If nothing changed in the next year, would you stay?

Healing Steps

P — **Set a timeline — not as an ultimatum, but as self-respect.**

O — **Know what commitment looks like for you. Know how long you're willing to wait. And honor that boundary.**

P — **Affirm Daily: "I will not stay in limbo. If he cannot choose me fully, he does not get access to me partially."**

Closing Truth

A man who sees your value does not risk losing you.

He does not keep you guessing.

He does not stall while benefiting from your loyalty.

Delayed commitment is not patience. It is permission.

We deserve progress. We deserve clarity.

We deserve commitment. We deserve more than potential.

The Truth:

When a man leaves you in He never fully leaves.

But he never fully chooses you either.

You are not single.

But you are not secure.

The Truth:

**When a man keeps you in limbo,
he is not confused
— he is comfortable.**

PART 3:

THE PATTERN

What's Really Happening.

The Shift from Confusion to Awareness.

Chapter Nine

Emotional Unavailability — He's Here, But He's Not Present

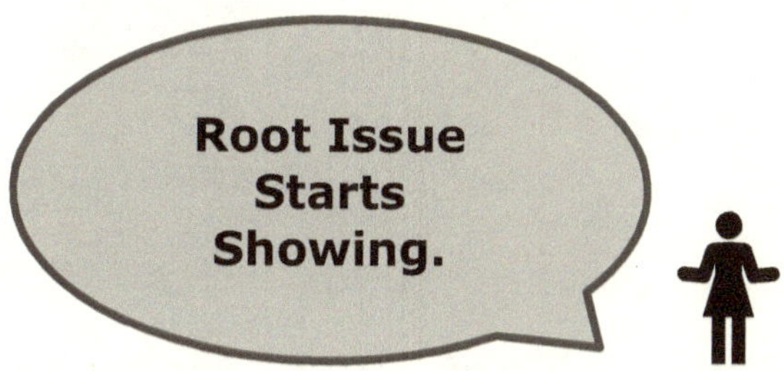

He is sitting right next to you, but it feels like he is miles away.

His body is there, but his heart, his mind, his spirit — all absent.

You share your feelings, your fears, your dreams, and he nods, even says the right words, but you know he is not there. His eyes drift. His energy pulls back. You leave the conversation emptier than when you started.

This is emotional unavailability: when a man gives you his presence without connection. When he offers you a body, but not a heart. When he exists in the relationship, but never truly shows up for it.

Red Flag: If vulnerability feels one-sided, you are in a relationship with a wall, not a partner.

The Silence That Hurts More Than Words

It is not always what he says that breaks you — it is what he does not say.

The unanswered texts. The one-word responses. The way he changes the subject when things get "too deep."

At first, you tell yourself he is just private, just guarded, just not used to opening up. You convince yourself that if you love him hard enough, he will eventually let you in. But months pass, even years, and he never does.

The BS They Tell Us

■ Lines of the Emotionally Unavailable Man:
- "I'm just not good at talking about my feelings."
- "That's just how I am."

- "You're too emotional, I don't get like that."
- "I am here, aren't I? Isn't that enough?"

Translation:

Words	Actions
"I'm just not good at talking about my feelings."	"I don't want to try, because this works for me."
"That's just how I am."	"I refuse to grow or stretch beyond my comfort zone."
"You're too emotional."	"I want you to shrink your needs, so I don't have to step up."
"Isn't that enough?"	"I want credit for showing up halfway."

Why We Stay

> You found yourself explaining his behavior
>
> more than he ever did.
>
> And somehow, that started to feel normal.

We stay because emotional crumbs feel better than nothing at all. We stay because the idea of starting over is exhausting. We stay because we remember the rare times he did open up, and we cling to those moments like proof that more is possible.

But the truth? His silence is not temporary. His distance is not circumstantial. His walls are not accidents — they are choices. And every time you accept them, you teach him that he can keep them.

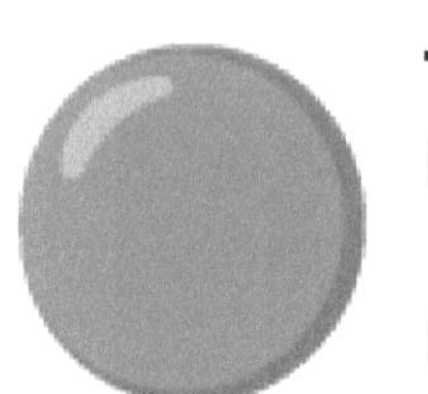

The Cost of Loving an Unavailable Man

Loving someone who will not open up costs you more than time. It costs you intimacy. It costs you peace. It costs you the deep, soul-level connection that every woman deserves.

- You start to believe intimacy means begging.
- You start silencing your needs because you don't want to "pressure" him.
- You learn to settle for surface-level conversations instead of real connection.
- You begin to think love is supposed to feel lonely.

But love is not supposed to feel like a locked door.

Red Flag Checklist

- He avoids serious conversations or changes the subject.
- He shuts down or withdraws when conflict arises.

• He only engages on a surface level — jokes, sex, small talk.
• You feel like you are always the one pushing for closeness.
• You feel lonelier with him than without him.

Reflection Prompts

1. Think of the last time you shared something vulnerable. How did he respond?
2. How often do you feel emotionally safe and heard in your relationship?
3. If you stopped asking him to open up, would intimacy still exist between you?

Healing Steps

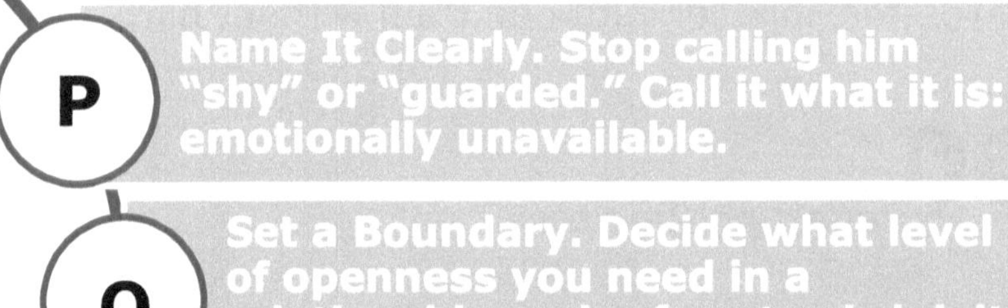

Closing Truth

An emotionally unavailable man can share your bed, your home, even your life — but he will never share himself. And that is not love, that's proximity.

If you are begging for intimacy, starving for connection, and silencing yourself to avoid being "too much," you are not loved — you are tolerated.

We are not tolerating half-love anymore. We are not settling for men who hide behind silence. We are not confusing proximity with partnership. Because we do not just deserve someone who is there.

We deserve someone who is present. We deserve connection. We deserve more than potential.

The Truth:

Presence without connection is loneliness in disguise.

Chapter Ten

Bare Minimum Effort — Loving You Only When You Complain

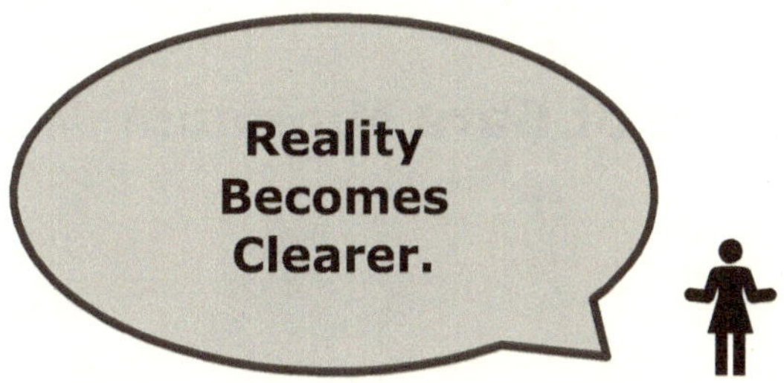

You should not have to beg to be loved properly.

But with the bare minimum man, love only shows up when you are ready to walk out the door. He does not buy flowers unless it is after an argument. He does not plan dates unless you remind him. He does not check in unless you have already broken down in tears.

And every time you call him out, suddenly he becomes the man you have been waiting for. For a week. Two. Then the cycle resets.

Red Flag: If effort only arrives when you complain, it is not effort — it is survival. He is not showing up because he values you, he is showing up because he fears losing access to you.

The Cycle of Bare Minimum

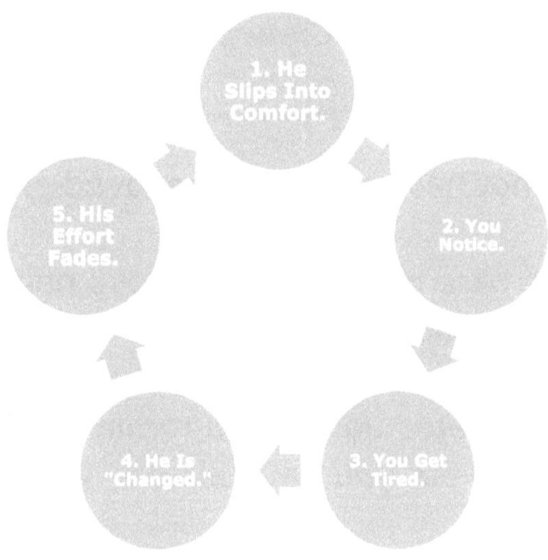

Here is how it goes:

1. He slips into comfort. Stops doing the trivial things. Stops showing appreciation. Stops putting in real effort.
2. You notice. You bring it up. He accuses you of nagging.
3. You get tired. You stop fighting, but your silence screams.
4. Suddenly, he is "changed." He is attentive,

romantic, consistent — for a little while.
5. Once he feels safe again, the effort fades. Back to step one. This cycle can last years if you let it. Years of begging for scraps and calling them meals.

 The BS They Tell Us

■ Bare Minimum Excuses:

- "I've just been busy, but you know how I feel."
- "Why do you always want so much? Isn't what I do enough?"
- "I'll do better, I promise."
- "You're making a big deal out of nothing."

Translation:

Words	Actions
"I've been busy."	"I didn't prioritize you."
"Why do you want so much?"	"I don't want to grow, so I'll guilt you for expecting better."
"I'll do better"	"I'll do the minimum until you stop being mad."
"You're making a big deal."	"I don't want to be held accountable."

Why We Stay

> It wasn't nothing.
>
> But it wasn't everything either.
>
> And you stayed, trying to convince yourself it was enough.

Because we are taught to be grateful.

Because we convince ourselves at least he tries. Because those short bursts of effort feel like proof that he really does care.

But here is the truth: Love that only shows up under pressure is not love. It is maintenance. It's damage control. It is keeping you quiet long enough so he can go back to doing less.

And bare minimum love is dangerous — because it conditions you to believe that your needs are "too much."

The Cost of Accepting Bare Minimum Love

- You start celebrating crumbs like they are full meals.
- You stop asking for what you really want because you do not want to feel needy.

- You train yourself to lower your standards just to keep the peace.
- You lose sight of what true partnership even looks like.

The longer you accept bare minimum love, the more you shrink yourself to fit it.

Red Flag Checklist

- He only steps up when you are angry or threatening to leave.
- You feel more relief than joy when he does the "right thing."
- His love feels like a reward for silence instead of a constant presence.
- You are always the one reminding, asking, or begging for effort.

Reflection Prompts

1. Think of the last time he "stepped up." Did it last, or did it fade once you calmed down?
2. Write down three ways you have accepted crumbs and called it love.
3. What would it feel like to have effort that was consistent, not conditional?

Healing Steps

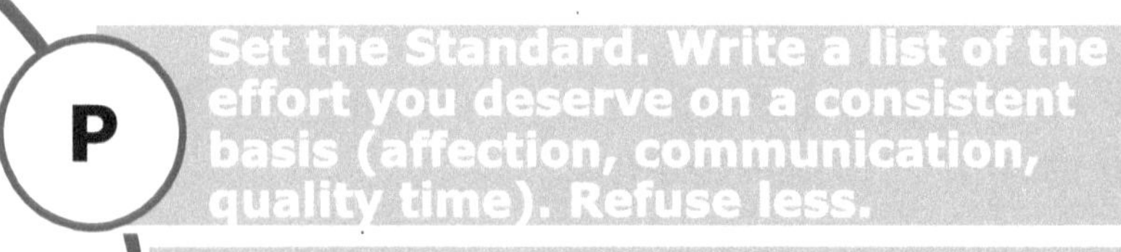

O

Stop Applauding Bare Minimum. Do not celebrate a man doing what he should have been doing all along.

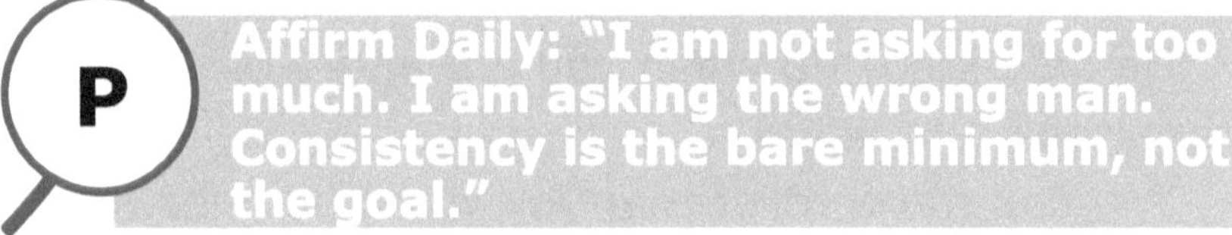

Closing Truth

The bare minimum is not enough. Love is not something you beg for. Effort is not something you chase.

If his effort only shows up when you are on the edge of leaving, that is not love — that's manipulation.

Because a man who truly values you will not wait for a complaint to treat you right. He'll do it every day, without needing to be reminded. We are not settling for crumbs anymore. We are not begging for basics.

We are not shrinking to fit inside half-love. Because we do not just deserve better. We deserve fullness. We deserve peace. We deserve more than potential.

The Truth:

A man who truly values you will treat you right every day.

Chapter Eleven

Excuses / Justification — Empty Apologies Does Not Mean Change

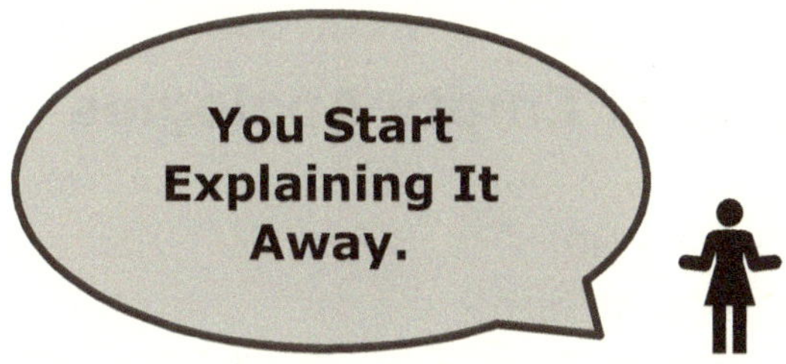

He says he is sorry. Sorry for forgetting, sorry for lying, sorry for breaking your trust.

And in that moment, the words soothe you. They give you hope. They convince you that he finally understands how much he's hurt you.

But then — he does it again. And again. And again.

Red Flag: An apology without change is just manipulation. Real apologies come with transformation, not repetition.

The Cycle of Empty Apologies

1. He messes up.
2. You confront him.
3. He says, "I'm sorry, it won't happen again."
4. You forgive.
5. He repeats the same behavior.

This cycle does not mean he does not know better. It means he does not care enough to do better.

The BS They Tell Us

■ Classic Empty Lines:

- "I said I was sorry, what more do you want?"
- "Nobody's perfect, stop expecting too much."
- "You always bring up the past."
- "I didn't mean to, it just happened."

Translation:

Words	Actions
"What more do you want?"	"I want forgiveness without accountability."
"Nobody's perfect."	"I want you to excuse my patterns."
"Stop bringing up the past."	"I do not want to be reminded of my repeated failures."
"It just happened."	"I do not want to admit my choices are intentional."

Why We Stay

> You kept replaying conversations in your head.
>
> Trying to understand something
>
> that never felt clear to begin with.

Because we want to believe the apology is real.

Because we've seen glimpses of him trying, and we hold on to those moments.

Because "sorry" feels like progress in the moment — even when it is not backed by action.

But here is the truth: "Sorry" does not heal wounds. Change does.

The Cost of Empty Apologies

- You become numb to his words.
- You start lowering your expectations.
- You begin accepting cycles of harm as "normal."
- You lose faith in your own standards because he keeps moving the goalposts.

The cost is your trust.

Once trust erodes, love cannot stand.

Red Flag Checklist

- He repeats the same mistakes no matter how many times he apologizes.
- His apologies feel rushed or defensive.
- You forgive without ever seeing proof of change.
- You feel like the only one holding him accountable.

Reflection Prompts

1. When was the last time his apology actually resulted in changed behavior?
2. How often have you forgiven the same mistake?
3. If your daughter or sister told you this story, would you tell her to accept "sorry" again?

Healing Steps

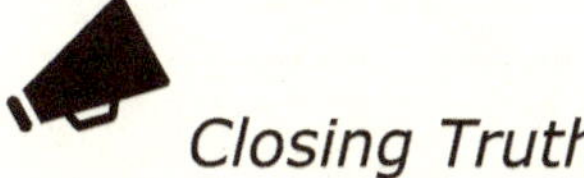

Closing Truth

Apologies should be bridges, not band-aids. They should lead to repair, not repetition. They should rebuild trust, not reset the cycle.

If his "sorry" is the only effort he ever gives, that's not accountability — that's survival.

And survival is not love.

We are not forgiving without transformation anymore.

We are not excusing patterns with words anymore.

We are not confusing apologies with progress anymore.

Because we do not just deserve "sorry."

We deserve change. We deserve growth. We deserve more than potential.

The Truth:

Apologies should be bridges, not band-aids.

Chapter Twelve

Confusion as a Pattern — Are You Asking the Wrong Man?

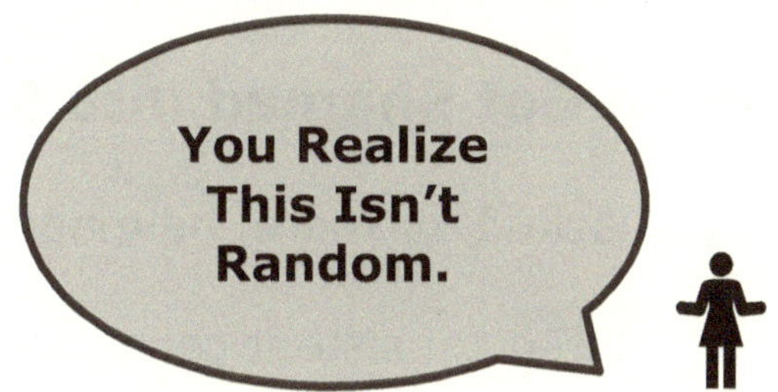

They told you you are too emotional.

Too sensitive.

Too needy.

Too much.

But let us be clear: asking for honesty, consistency, effort, communication, and love that shows up every day is not asking for too much. It is simply asking for the basics. The fact that he could always give it to you does not make you excessive — it makes him unqualified.

Red Flag: If someone makes you feel guilty for wanting the basics, they cannot give you real love.

How Women Get Shamed into Silence

Every time you asked for more, he made you feel guilty.
• When you wanted consistent communication, he said you were clingy.
• When you asked for quality time, he said you were demanding.
• When you wanted clarity, he called you dramatic.
• When you asked for reassurance, he accused you of being insecure.

The pattern is always the same: he minimizes your needs, so he does not have to meet them.

 The BS They Tell Us

■ Classic Lines:
• "You expect too much from me."
• "Why can't you just relax and go with the flow?"
• "Other women would be happy with what I give."
• "You're always complaining."

Translation:

Words	Actions
"You expect too much."	"I do not want to grow beyond my comfort zone."
"Go with the flow."	"I want a relationship without responsibility."
"Other women…"	"I want to guilt you into settling."
"You're always complaining."	"I do not want to be accountable for my lack of effort."

Why We Stay

> You saw who he *could be*.
>
> And held onto that
>
> more than who he actually was.

Because society tells us men are simple, and women are complicated.

Because we don't want to be "the nag." Because we start to believe that our standards really are too high.

But here is the truth:
You are not asking for too much. You are asking the wrong person.

The Cost of Shrinking Your Needs

Every time you silence your needs, you shrink yourself.

- You stop asking for communication and learn to live with silence.
- You stop asking for quality time and learn to live with neglect.
- You stop asking for clarity and learn to live with confusion.
- You stop asking for reassurance and learn to live with doubt. And in the process, you start convincing yourself that crumbs are meals.

Red Flag Checklist

- He makes you feel guilty for asking for consistency.
- He calls you "too emotional" when you want communication.
- He compares you to other women instead of loving you as you are.
- You feel punished every time you express a need.

Reflection Prompts

1. What is one thing you have been told you "Expect too much" about?
2. How has silencing that need hurt your peace?
3. What would it feel like to be with someone who saw your needs as natural, not excessive?

Healing Steps

P — **Redefine "Too Much." Write down the needs you have been shamed for and recognize them as valid.**

O — **Stop Apologizing. You do not need to apologize for needing love, communication, or consistency.**

P — **Affirm Daily: "I am not too much. I am just not for the wrong man. The right one will call my standards his own."**

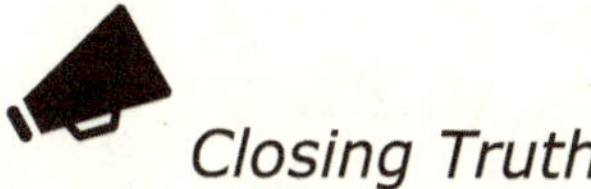

Closing Truth

A man who calls you "too much" is a man who does not have enough to give.

Your needs are not excessive — they are the blueprint for healthy love.

Stop silencing yourself. Stop shrinking your voice. Stop apologizing for your truth.

Because you were never too much. You were always enough — he just was not.

And the right man? He will see your needs not as demands, but as opportunities to love you better.

We are not lowering our standards anymore. We are not apologizing for our needs anymore. We are not shrinking anymore.

Because we do not just deserve potential.

We deserve real love. Consistent love. Love that meets us where we are and does not ask us to apologize for needing it.

The Truth:

The right man will not negotiate your needs — he will meet them.

PART 4:

THE INTERNAL SHIFT

Turning Inward.

Going Deeper Emotionally.

Chapter Thirteen

Overgiving — When "Protection" Feels Like Possession

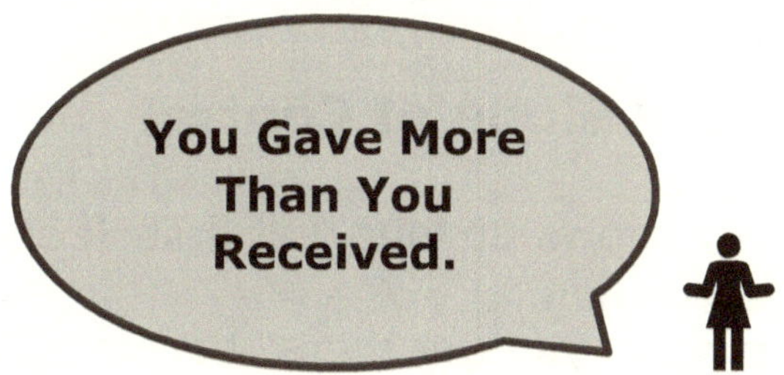

At first, it sounds sweet.

He says he just wants to know where you are because he "cares." He wants you to text when you get home because he "worries." He wants you to dress a certain way because he "respects you." But slowly, the care starts to feel like control.

Suddenly, you are asking permission instead of sharing plans. You are adjusting your wardrobe to avoid arguments.

You are cutting off friends because he does not "like their influence."

Red Flag: When love starts to feel like restriction, it's not love — its control dressed as concern.

The Slippery Slope of Control

Control rarely shows up loudly at first. It sneaks in, wrapped in affection.

- "Text me when you get there" becomes "don't go there without me."
- "I don't like it when you talk to him" becomes "block him right now."
- "I want you safe" becomes "I want to know where you are at all times."

It doesn't feel suffocating until one day you realize you can't breathe.

 The BS They Tell Us

■ What controlling men say to mask it as love:

- "I just want what's best for you."
- "I'm only like this because I care."
- "If you loved me, you wouldn't want to do that anyway."
- "I'm protecting what's mine."

Translation:

Words	Actions
"What's best for you."	"I want to decide your life for you."
"Because I care."	"I use love as an excuse for control."
"If you loved me..."	"I want you to feel guilty for wanting freedom."
"You're mine."	"I see you as possession, not a partner."

Why We Stay

> You gave more.
>
> More time. More understanding. More patience.
>
> Hoping eventually,
>
> it would be returned.

Because in the beginning, control feels like attention.

Because we mistake possessiveness for passion. Because we're told a jealous man is just a man who loves hard.

But here's the truth: Jealousy is not love. Possession is not protection. And restriction is not care.

The Cost of Staying with Control

- You begin shrinking your life to avoid conflict.
- You lose friendships, hobbies, and pieces of yourself.
- You confuse fear with love.
- You stop recognizing your own freedom.

The cost of control is your independence. And without independence, there can be no true love.

Red Flag Checklist

- He checks your phone, messages, or social media without permission.
- He makes you feel guilty for having a life outside of him.
- He uses "love" to justify jealousy or possessiveness.
- You feel more restricted than supported.

Reflection Prompts

1. What freedoms have you given up in the name of "keeping the peace"?
2. Do his rules make you feel loved, or trapped?
3. What would it look like to be with someone who encouraged your freedom instead of restricting it?

Healing Steps

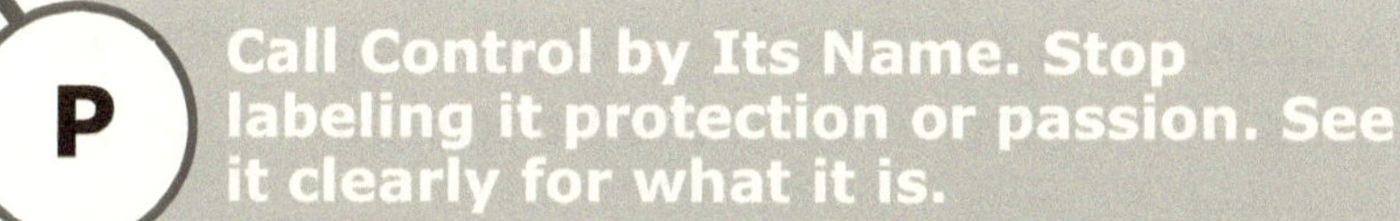

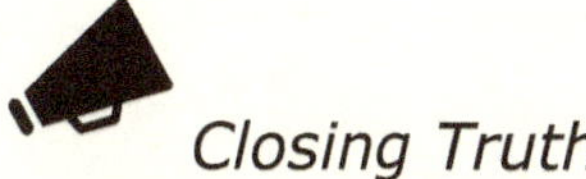

Closing Truth

Love is not about ownership. It's about freedom, choice, and mutual respect. A man who truly loves you will not clip your wings — he will help you fly.

Don't let control hide under the mask of concern.

Don't let "protection" silence your independence.

Don't let love become a prison. We are not trading freedom for love anymore. We are not confusing control with care anymore.

We are not mistaking jealousy for passion anymore.

Because we don't just deserve to be kept.

We deserve to be chosen — freely, daily, without chains. We deserve more than potential.

The Truth:

**When love starts to feel like restriction,
it's not love
— its control dressed as concern.**

Chapter Fourteen

Ignoring the Red Flags — Gaslighting

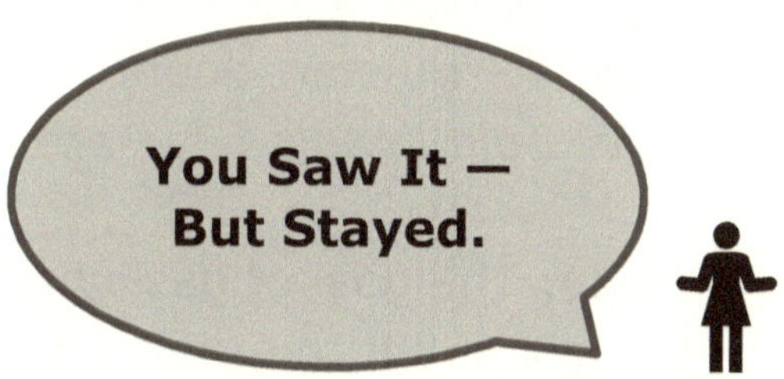

Gaslighting is one of the most dangerous red flags because it does not just hurt you — it makes you question yourself. It is not always loud, not always violent. Sometimes it is quiet, subtle, disguised as concern, until suddenly you do not trust your own voice anymore.

It starts with a disagreement. You mention something that hurt you, something you noticed, something that does not sit right. Instead of addressing it, he flips it back on you.

You say: "It hurt when you ignored my calls."
He says: "You are overreacting. I was busy."

You say: "I saw those messages. That crossed a line."
He says: "You are being paranoid. That is not even what happened."

You say: "I feel like I can't trust you."
He says: "You are too sensitive. You make problems where there are none."

At first, you argue. You try to prove your case, to show evidence, to explain your feelings. But after a while, you get tired. You start doubting yourself. *I am too sensitive. I did imagine it. I am the problem.*

Red Flag: The goal of gaslighting is not to fix the issue, but to erase your confidence that the issue even existing.

The Poison of Gaslighting

Gaslighting is emotional manipulation at its core. It shifts the blame away from him and drops it into your lap. It is not about truth — it is about control.

The poison of gaslighting is that it works slowly. You do not wake up one morning doubting yourself; it builds drop by drop:

- A denial here.
- A twisted story there.
- A casual "you're crazy" said in a laughing tone.

Before long, you do not recognize yourself. You are quiet where you used to speak. You are doubtful where you used to trust your instincts. You apologize for things you did not do just to keep the peace.

Red Flag: If every conversation leaves you feeling like you are the problem, you are not in love — you are being manipulated.

The BS They Tell Us

■ Gaslighter's Greatest Hits:

- "You're crazy."
- "That never happened.".
- "You're imagining things."
- "Nobody else would put up with you."
- "You're too emotional."

Translation:

Words	Actions
"You're crazy."	"I do not want to take responsibility."
"That never happened."	"I am rewriting history, so I don't look guilty."
"You're imagining things."	"I know the truth, but I don't want to admit it."
"Nobody else would put up with you."	"I want you to feel trapped."
"You're too emotional."	"I want you to stop calling out my behavior."

These are not harmless comments. These are strategies. Each line is designed to chip away at your reality until you are left living inside his version of the truth.

Why We Stay

> You stopped saying what you needed.
>
> Not because it didn't matter—
>
> but because you didn't want to lose him.

We do not believe gaslighting because we are weak — we believe it because we love. Love makes us want to see the best. Love makes us want to forgive.

Love makes us want to think, he is right, I just misunderstood.

And for women especially, we have been conditioned to doubt ourselves.

Society calls us "too emotional," "too needy," "too dramatic." When a man we love says the same thing, it hits harder.

So, we silence ourselves. We shrink. We stop listening to the voice inside that says, this isn't right.

The Cost of Gaslighting

Gaslighting does not just make you doubt him — it makes you doubt yourself.

- You stop trusting your memory.
- You stop trusting your feelings.
- You stop trusting your instincts.

The cost is self-betrayal. Every time you accept his version of events over your own, you abandon yourself a little more. And the longer it goes on, the harder it is to leave, because you're not even sure what is anymore.

But here is the truth: If your heart, your gut, and your spirit all scream something is wrong — it is wrong!

Red Flag Checklist

- He denies things you know happened.
- He calls you crazy, sensitive, or dramatic when you express pain.
- He makes you feel guilty for confronting him.
- You leave conversations feeling confused, not heard.
- You start apologizing just to end arguments.

Reflection Prompts

1. Think back to the last argument where you walked away confused. What did he say that made you doubt yourself?
2. Write down three moments where your instincts told you one thing, but he convinced you it was something else.
3. Ask yourself: If your best friend told you the same story, would you believe her or blame her?

Healing Steps

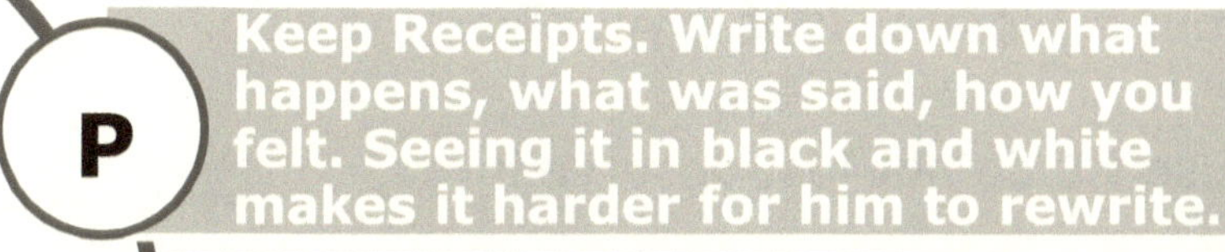

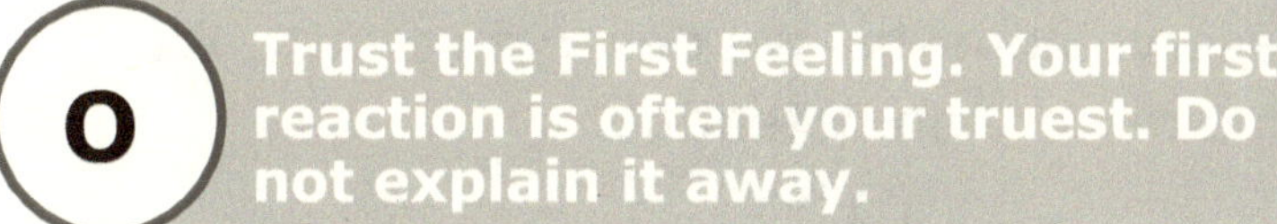

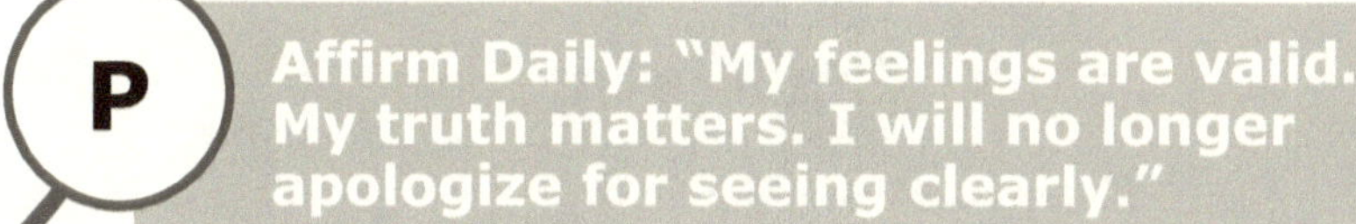

Closing Truth

Gaslighting is not love.
Love listens. Love takes accountability. Love honors your feelings even when it does not understand them.

If every argument leaves you doubting yourself, that's not miscommunication — that's manipulation.

And the most dangerous thing about gaslighting is that it convinces you to silence yourself. But silence is not survival. Silence is surrender. We are not surrendering anymore. We are not shrinking anymore. We are not settling anymore.

When a man makes you doubt your reality; that is not your soulmate. That is your warning sign.

Because we do not just deserve love.

We deserve honesty. We deserve respect. We deserve more than potential.

The Truth:

Gaslighting
does not just make you doubt him
— it makes you doubt yourself.

Chapter Fifteen

Dependency of Emotional Labor — You Are Doing All the Work

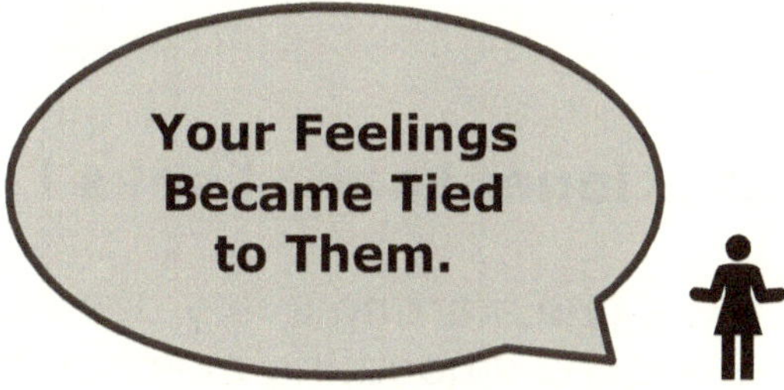

You carry it all. The check-ins. The "good morning" texts. The remembering of birthdays, anniversaries, the tiny details that keep a relationship alive. The emotional glue that holds the connection together — it is always you.

He leans on your strength but never offers his. He vents to you, unloads on you, expects you to listen — but when it is your turn, suddenly he is "too tired" or "not in the mood."

Red Flag: If you are always the giver and rarely the receiver, you are not in a partnership — you are in a one-sided relationship disguised as love.

What Emotional Labor Looks Like

- You are the one starting every deep conversation.
- You are the one smoothing over conflicts.
- You are the one noticing shifts in energy and trying to fix them.
- You are the one carrying his emotional baggage while yours goes untouched.

This is not love. This is parenting. And you were not built to mother a grown man.

 The BS They Tell Us

■ Excuses Men Use to Dodge Emotional Effort:

- "That's just how I am, I don't talk about feelings."
- "You're better at that stuff than me."
- "I didn't know it was a big deal."
- "You always want to argue."

Translation:

Words	Actions
"That's how I am."	"I do not want to grow."
"You're better at that."	"I want you to do all the work while I stay comfortable."
"It's not a big deal."	"Your needs are not important to me."
"You always want to argue."	"I would rather silence you than listen to you."

Why We Stay

> You saw the signs early.
>
> But you told yourself
>
> they weren't that serious.

Because we are natural nurturers. Because we are told women should be the backbone. Because society teaches us those men "don't do feelings" and it is our job to pick up the slack.

But here is the truth: Emotional labor in a healthy relationship is shared. Love is not a one-way transaction.

The Cost of Carrying It All

- You grow resentful while he grows comfortable.
- You start to feel more like his therapist than his partner.
- You silence your own needs because you are too busy meeting his.
- You burn out emotionally and physically while he thrives on your energy.

The cost of doing all the emotional work is simple: you disappear while he stays whole.

Red Flag Checklist

- You are the one always fixing the relationship.
- He shuts down when you bring up your feelings.
- You know more about his emotions than he knows about yours.
- You feel drained while he feels supported.

Reflection Prompts

1. When was the last time he checked in on you without you asking?
2. How often do your emotional needs get prioritized compared to his?

3. What would it feel like if someone poured into you the way you pour into others?

Healing Steps

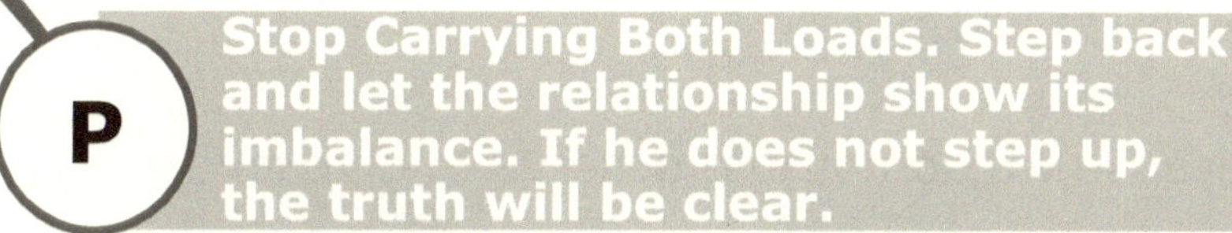

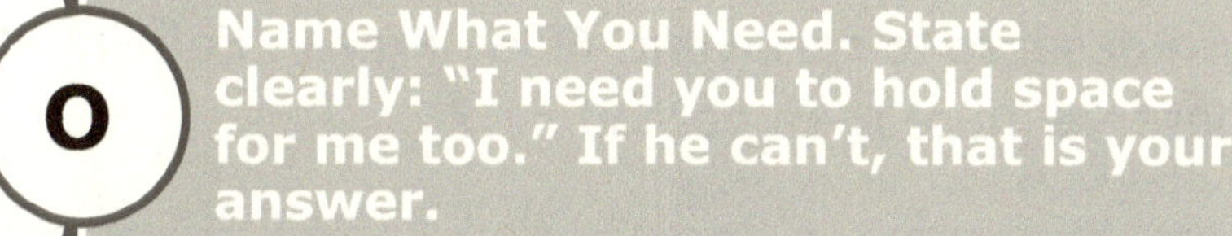

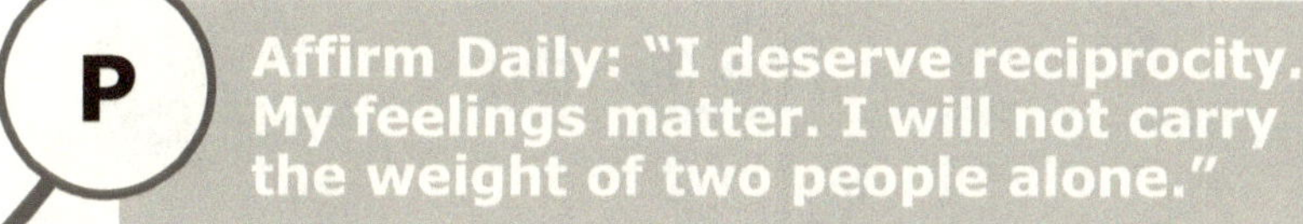

Closing Truth

Relationships are not meant to drain you. You were not built to be a man's emotional crutch.

You deserve someone who notices your tears without you having to explain, who checks in just because, who holds space for your storms as much as you hold space for his.

If you are always the giver and rarely the receiver, that's not partnership. That's exploitation.

We are not mothering grown men anymore.

We are not silencing our needs to carry someone else's anymore. We are not confusing strength with servitude anymore.

Because we do not just deserve to give love.

We deserve to receive it. Fully. Freely. Equally. We deserve more than potential.

The Truth:

If you are always the giver and rarely the receiver,
you are not in a partnership
— you are in a one-sided relationship

Chapter Sixteen

Self-Abandonment — Cheating Is Not a Mistake It is a Choice

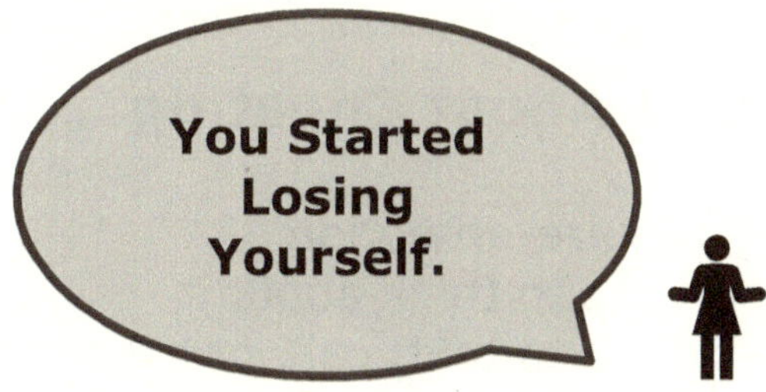

He will say it was a slip-up. A weak moment. A mistake.

But let us be clear: cheating is not something that just "happens." It is not tripping on a sidewalk. It is not forgetting your keys. It is a deliberate decision to betray the person who trusted you.

Red Flag: When a man cheats and minimizes it, he is not sorry for hurting you — he's sorry for getting caught.

The Truth About Cheating

Cheating requires intention.
- He had time to think about it.
- He had time to text, call, or meet her.
- He had time to decide if your love mattered enough to stay faithful.

And every step of the way, he chose betrayal.

That is not weakness. That is not an accident. That is a choice.

The BS They Tell Us

■ Excuses of a Cheater:
- "It didn't mean anything."
- "It was just physical."
- "You weren't giving me what I needed."
- "I love you; it was just a mistake."

Translation:

Words	Actions
"It didn't mean anything."	"I want you to think betrayal is less painful if it is casual."
"Just physical."	"I want to downplay the emotional wound."
"You weren't giving me..."	"I want to make you responsible for my choice to cheat."
"It was a mistake."	"I want forgiveness without accountability."

Why We Stay

> Your mood started to depend on him.
>
> When he was there, you felt okay.
>
> When he wasn't—you felt it.

Because the apologies sound convincing. Because we do not want to start over. Because we hope the betrayal was a one-time thing. Because society tells women to "fight for their man" even when he is the one who betrayed them.

But the truth? Cheating is not about lack of opportunity — it is about lack of respect.

The Cost of Accepting Cheating

- You begin to internalize his betrayal as your failure.
- You live in constant anxiety, checking phones, overanalyzing everything.
- You lose trust — not just in him, but in yourself.
- You teach him that your forgiveness is guaranteed.

The cost of tolerating cheating is your peace. And your peace is priceless.

Red Flag Checklist

- He blames you for why he cheated.
- He minimizes the betrayal instead of owning it.
- You find yourself policing him instead of trusting him.
- He repeats the behavior after being forgiven.

Reflection Prompts

1. What excuse did he give for cheating — and why did you believe it?
2. How has betrayal changed the way you see yourself?

3. If someone else told you this story, what would you tell her to do?

Healing Steps

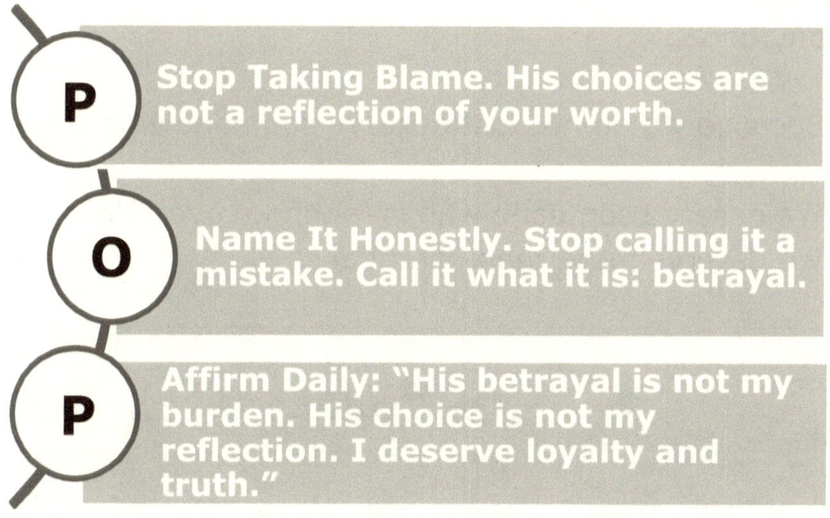

Closing Truth

Cheating does not happen by accident. It happens by decision. And every time he cheats, he decides your heart is not worth his discipline.

Do not let a man convince you that his betrayal is your responsibility.

Don't let him shrink the pain of infidelity into something you should "just get over."

Do not let him break you, then call it love.

We are not excusing betrayal anymore.

We are not accepting infidelity as "normal" anymore.

We are not confusing apologies with accountability anymore.

Because we do not just deserve someone who stays.

We deserve someone who is faithful. Loyal. Honest. We deserve more than potential.

The Truth:

Cheating is not something that just "happens." It is choice. It is a deliberate decision to betray the person who trusted you.

PART 5:

THE BREAK

Transformation.

This is the turning point + empowerment.

Chapter Seventeen

Losing Yourself, Reclaiming Your Power — Coming Home to Yourself

Somewhere along the way, you forgot who you were. Not because you were weak, but because you were surviving. Not because you did not love yourself, but because you poured so much love into him, you had none left for you.

You gave pieces of yourself away in exchange for his half-effort. You shrunk your voice, so his comfort stayed intact.

You carried both his weight and yours because you believed love was sacrifice, even if it meant losing yourself.

Red Flag: You give more of yourself away than you have. Now, it is time to come home to you.

The Power You Gave Away

Power does not leave all at once. It seeps out in small moments:

- When you let him dismiss your feelings because you did not want to argue.
- When you lowered your standards to "keep the peace."
- When you apologized for needs that were reasonable.
- When you stayed quiet to avoid being labeled dramatic.

One by one, those moments add up until you look in the mirror and wonder, where did I go?

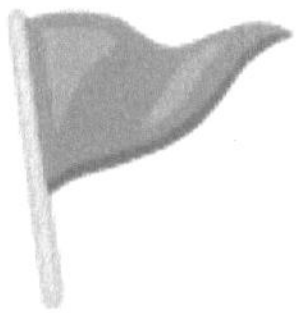

Red Flag: If you no longer recognize yourself in the relationship, you have given away too much.

The BS They Tell Us

■ What steals your power:

- "You are lucky I stayed. No one else would deal with you."
- "You're overthinking — it's not that serious."
- "Why can't you just be happy with what we have?"
- "You're making me out to be the bad guy."

Translation:

Words	Actions
"No one else would deal with you."	"I want you to believe you cannot do better."
"It's not that serious."	"I do not want to face my behavior."
"Be happy with what we have."	"Settle for my convenience."
"Stop making me the bad guy."	"Do not hold me accountable."

Why We Stay

You started adjusting.

Your expectations. Your reactions. Yourself.

Until you barely recognized

how much you had changed.

We are taught that love is endurance. That a good woman "holds her man down" no matter what.

That loyalty means sacrificing your happiness for the sake of keeping a relationship.

But here is the truth: Loyalty without reciprocity is not love. It's slavery. And you were never meant to be chained to someone else's immaturity.

The Cost of Losing Yourself

- You start doubting your worth outside of him.
- You silence your needs until you do not even know them anymore.
- You trade your power for his validation.
- You become a shadow of yourself instead of the full woman you were created to be.

But the cost is not final — because power is never lost. It is waiting for you to pick it back up.

Red Flag Checklist

- You apologize for things you did not do just to keep peace.
- You feel smaller in the relationship than you did before it.

- You cannot remember the last time you decided for yourself.
- You feel more drained than empowered when he is around.

Reflection Prompts

1. What is one boundary you have let slide that you wish you had held firm?
2. In what ways have you made yourself smaller to keep the relationship alive?
3. What does "coming home to yourself" look like in your daily life?

Healing Steps

P — **Set a Boundary and Keep It. Get clear. Power is rebuilt every time you say no without apology.**

O — **Reintroduce Yourself to You. Write down what makes you feel alive outside of a relationship. Reclaim it.**

P — **Affirm Daily: "I am whole. I am enough. I am not shrinking anymore — I am returning to myself."**

Closing Truth

Reclaiming your power is not about becoming someone new. It's about remembering who you were before you handed your strength to someone who didn't know how to honor it.

You are not lost. You are not broken. You are not too far gone.

You are simply coming home — to your voice, to your peace, to your truth.

And when you stand in that power again, *you'll realize the truth:* You were never asking for too much.

You were worthy.

You were simply giving your best to someone who could not hold it. Now, you are holding it for yourself.

Because we do not just deserve to survive love.

We deserve to thrive in it. We deserve to rise in it. We deserve more than potential.

The Truth:

Reclaiming your power is not about becoming someone new. It's about remembering who you are.

Take a moment and reflect on these questions:

What did I tolerate?

What Will I never tolerate again?

Chapter Eighteen

The Turning Point — Choosing Solitude Over Chaos

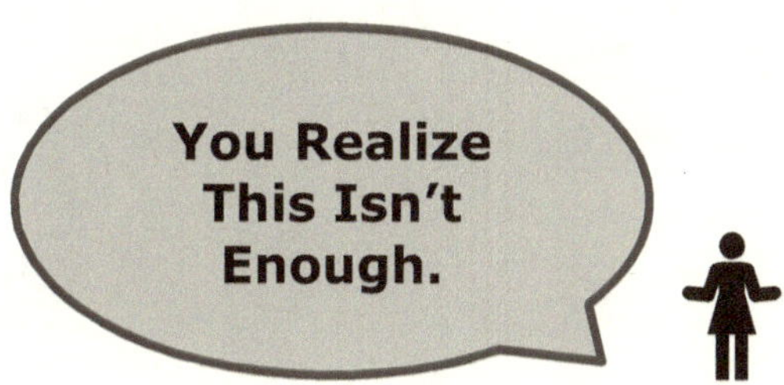

Loneliness is dangerous. Not because being alone will break you, but because loneliness will whisper lies when you are tired enough to believe them.

It tells you:
"Almost love is better than no love." "Red flags are just flaws you can fix."

"At least he's here sometimes — that's better than nothing."

And in the quiet hours of the night, when your bed feels too big and your heart feels too heavy, those lies sound convincing. That is how loneliness traps us in half-love — because almost feels safer than empty.

Red Flag: Settling because you are lonely is still settling. And loneliness is easier to heal than betrayal, manipulation, or neglect.

The Illusion of Almost

Loneliness makes crumbs look like meals.

- He texts occasionally, and you cling to it like proof of care.
- He shows up occasionally, and you convince yourself it is consistency.
- He says "I love you" without showing it, and you hold on because at least someone is saying the words.

But "almost" is not love. "Almost" is just a slower heartbreak.

The BS They Tell Us

■ What men feed you when they know you are afraid to be alone:

- "I'm not perfect, but at least I'm here."

- "You'll never find someone who puts up with you like I do."
- "Nobody wants to be alone, so why throw this away?"
- "We have our problems, but every relationship does."

Translation:

Words	Actions
"At least I'm here."	"Presence without effort."
"You'll never find better."	"Fear as control."
"Nobody wants to be alone."	"I am betting you will settle out of fear."
"Every relationship has problems."	"I want you to normalize dysfunction."

Why We Stay

> Nothing big happened.
>
> Just a quiet moment
>
> where you realized...
>
> this wasn't enough anymore.

Because loneliness is loud. Because the silence feels unbearable. Because we fear starting over, wondering if anyone else will choose us.

But here is the truth: There are worse things than being alone. And one of them is staying in a relationship that starves you.

The Cost of Settling Out of Loneliness

- You lose time you cannot get back.
- You accept confusion as if it is better than peace.
- You numb yourself to red flags until they feel normal.
- You trade your healing for temporary company.

Loneliness is hard. But healing is harder when you have settled for someone who never deserved you.

Red Flag Checklist

- You are staying more out of fear of being alone than genuine love.
- You feel lonelier with him than without him.
- His presence does not comfort you — it confuses you.
- You convince yourself "at least I have someone,"

even when you are unhappy.

Reflection Prompts

1. When was the last time his presence made you feel less lonely?
2. Are you staying because you love him — or because you are afraid of leaving?
3. What would it look like to embrace solitude as healing instead of punishment?

Healing Steps

P — **Redefine Alone. Being alone does not mean unloved — it means you are creating space for what you deserve.**

O — **Fill Your Own Cup. Invest in friendships, passions, and self-care that remind you of your worth.**

P — **Affirm Daily: "I will not trade my peace for company. I would rather be whole alone than broken together."**

Closing Truth

Loneliness whispers, but peace shouts louder. When you choose solitude over chaos, you choose yourself. And you discover that you were never truly alone — you had you all along.

Do not let loneliness make your decisions. Do not confuse empty presence with real partnership. Do not settle for someone who gives you less than you give yourself.

Because we are not staying out of fear anymore. We are not shrinking to avoid silence anymore. We are not confusing company with care anymore.

Because we do not just deserve someone.

We deserve the right one. We deserve peace, not presence. We deserve more than potential.

The Truth:

"Silence vs Chaos"
Peaceful alone versus Painful together

Chapter Nineteen

Detaching — Love Should Not Hurt

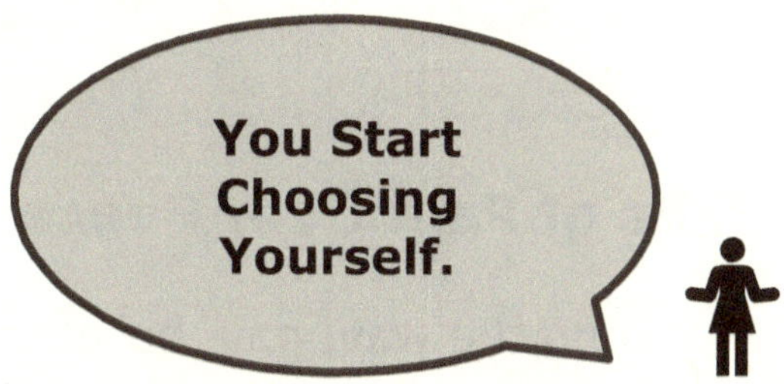

Some of us were raised to believe that love hurts. That it's supposed to break you before it builds you. That passion comes with pain. That if it doesn't cut deep, it's not real.

But here's the truth: Love was never meant to destroy you. Love is not supposed to feel like walking on eggshells.

Love is not supposed to leave scars.

Love is not supposed to steal your joy.

Red Flag: If the love you're in feels more like survival than safety, it's not love — it's trauma — wearing a disguise.

The Pitfalls of Pain Over Peace

Somewhere along the way, pain became familiar.

Not because you wanted it — but because you learned how to survive in it.

You learned how to:

- Stay when things didn't feel right.
- Justify behavior that hurt you.
- Normalize emotional inconsistency.
- Call chaos "passion" and instability "love".

And the longer you stayed, the more your nervous system adjusted.

Peace started to feel... unfamiliar.
Quiet felt uncomfortable.
Consistency felt boring.

So when love didn't hurt, you questioned it.
When someone showed up consistently, you waited for the other shoe to drop.

That is what happens when pain becomes your baseline.

But let's tell the truth:

Pain is not proof of love.
Struggle is not a requirement.
Confusion is not chemistry.

You were not meant to feel anxious in love.
You were not meant to question where you stand.
You were not meant to earn consistency.

You were conditioned to accept less — and call it normal.

But healing requires a new standard.

It requires choosing peace — even when it feels unfamiliar.

It requires walking away from what excites your wounds...and choosing what nurtures your growth.

Because love should not feel like something you survive.

It should feel like something you can rest in.

The BS They Tell Us

■ The Lies We Were Taught About Love

- "If he's jealous, it means he cares."
- "If it's hard, it's worth it."
- "No relationship is perfect — pain is normal."
- "Real love means enduring anything."

Translation:

Words	Actions
"Jealousy does not care."	"It's control."
"Constant struggle is not love."	"It's dysfunction."
"Pain is not normal."	"Respect, peace, and effort are."
"Endurance without reciprocity."	"It is slavery, not love."

Why We Stay

You didn't leave all at once.

You just started choosing yourself

in small ways—

until it became permanent.

Painful love is familiar. Because we confuse intensity with intimacy.

Because we believe struggle proves loyalty.

Because society glorifies women who "hold their man down" even when he's the one tearing her apart.

But let's be clear: Enduring abuse, betrayal, neglect, or manipulation doesn't make you stronger — it makes you a prisoner.

The Cost of Believing Love Should Hurt

- You normalize red flags as "just part of relationships."
- You lose the ability to recognize healthy love.
- You build tolerance for pain instead of boundaries for peace.
- You start believing that your suffering is proof of your love.

The cost is your future — because every day you stay in pain, you teach yourself that this is all you'll ever deserve.

Red Flag Checklist

- You cry more than you smile in the relationship.
- You excuse mistreatment as "part of love."
- You've convinced yourself pain means passion.
- You feel exhausted instead of safe.

Reflection Prompts

1. What messages about love did you grow up hearing — and how have they shaped what you accept now?
2. Do you, or have you, confused passion with pain in your current or past relationships?
3. What would love look like if peace, safety, and respect were your non-negotiables?

Healing Steps

P — **Redefine Love. Write down what love should feel like (peace, safety, respect, effort). Measure every relationship against it.**

O — **Reject Struggle Love. Stop glamorizing chaos and start demanding calm.**

P — **Affirm Daily: "Love is not supposed to break me. Real love heals, nurtures, and protects."**

Closing Truth

Love should never leave bruises — on your body, your mind, or your spirit. Love should not tear you apart to prove it's real. Love should not feel like a battlefield you barely survive.

If it hurts more than it heals, it's not love.

We are not glorifying struggle love anymore.

We are not normalizing pain as passion anymore.

We are not mistaking chaos for commitment anymore.

Because we do not just deserve to love.

We deserve to be loved in peace. In safety. In joy. We deserve more than potential.

The Truth:

Love was never meant to destroy you.
Love is not supposed to leave scars.
Love is not supposed to steal your joy.

Chapter Twenty

Final Realization — Choosing Yourself is the Highest Form of Love

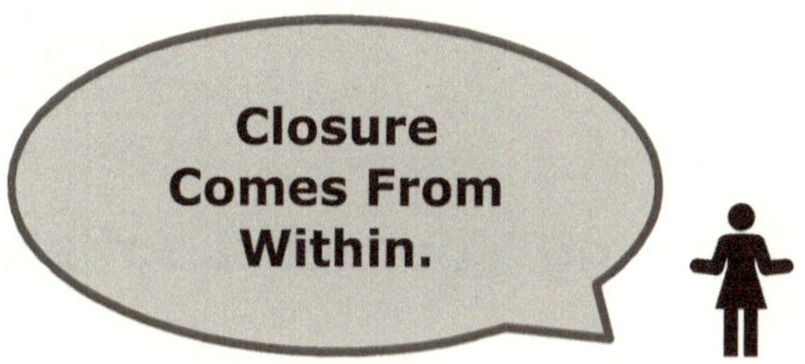

For so long, you have been told to choose him.

Choose patience.

Choose loyalty.

Choose sacrifice.

Even when it broke you. Even when it drained you. Even when it cost you your voice. But now? The cycle ends here.

Because the highest form of love you will ever experience is not from a man who can't meet you where you are — it's from you, finally choosing yourself.

Red Flag: When a relationship forces you to abandon yourself, it's no longer love — it's a warning to walk away.

What Choosing Yourself Looks Like

- Saying no without explaining.
- Walking away from half-effort.
- Refusing to wait on potential.
- Loving yourself loudly, daily, unapologetically.

Choosing yourself is not selfish.

It's sacred.

It's survival.

It's the foundation for every kind of healthy love that will come after.

The BS They Tell Us

■ What they say when you finally choose you:

- "You've changed."
- "You think you're too good now."

- "You'll never find someone like me."
- "You gave up too easily."

Translation:

Words	Actions
"You've changed."	"I can't control you anymore."
"Too good."	"You realized your worth and won't settle."
"Never find someone like me."	"And that's the point — you don't want to."
"Gave up."	"You stopped carrying what I refused to hold."

Why We Stay

> You didn't get closure from him.
>
> You got clarity from yourself.
>
> And that changed everything.

Choosing yourself matters because peace feels better than confusion. Because freedom feels better than possession. Because clarity feels better than potential. Often, we stay because it is what we know. The question becomes is it time to choose yourself. You matter.

And because the love you give yourself sets the standard for the love you allow from others.

The of Not Choosing Yourself

- You live in cycles of almost-love.
- You lose years waiting for change that never comes.
- You shrink your power for someone else's comfort.
- You forget that you were the prize all along.

The cost of abandoning yourself is always greater than the cost of walking away.

Red Flag Checklist

- You feel like you've lost yourself in the relationship.
- You prioritize his needs while ignoring your own.
- You stay out of fear instead of joy.
- You don't recognize your own reflection anymore.

Reflection Prompts

1. Where have you abandoned yourself to stay in love?
2. What does it mean for you to choose yourself fully right now?

3. What boundaries will you set to protect that choice moving forward?

Healing Steps

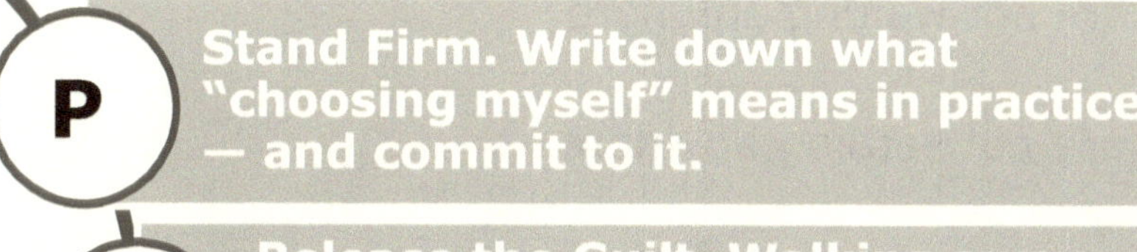

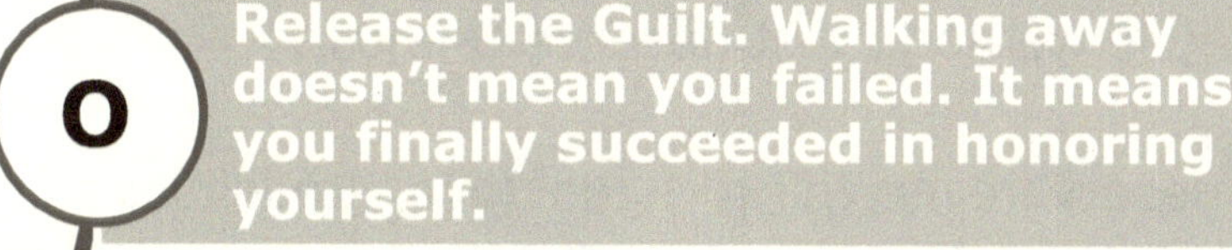

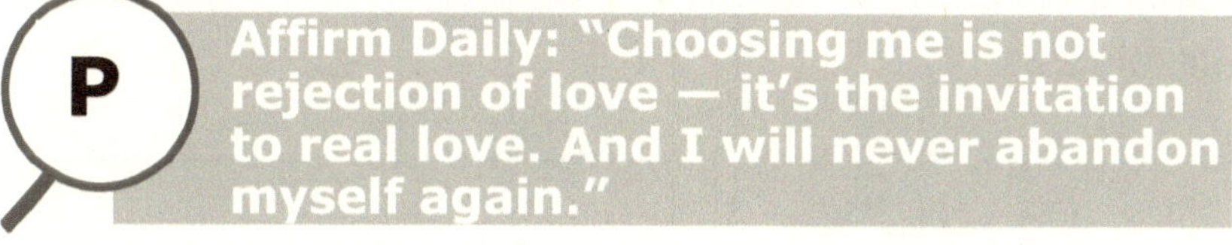

Closing Truth

This chapter is not the end — it's the beginning.

The beginning of a new standard.

The beginning of peace without apology.

The beginning of love that feels like freedom, not bondage.

Because choosing yourself is not the backup plan. It's the plan. It's the foundation. It's the only way to guarantee you'll never again settle for less than you deserve.

We are not shrinking anymore.

We are not waiting anymore.

We are not settling anymore.

Because we don't just deserve "almost."

We deserve everything — real love, steady love, healing love. And it starts with the love we give ourselves.

The Truth:

When a relationship forces you to abandon yourself, it's no longer love — it's a warning to walk away.

Epilogue

She Deserves More Than Potential — A Final Word

If you have made it this far, it means you are ready.

Ready to release the half-love.

Ready to stop chasing "someday."

Ready to stop confusing potential for proof.

Every chapter in this book was written as both a warning and a reminder.

A warning about the red flags we have been taught to excuse.

A reminder that you are worthy of love that does not require you to break yourself in half.

This is not just a book — it is a declaration. A declaration that women will no longer:

- Mother grown men.
- Apologize for our standards.
- Accept crumbs and call them meals.
- Confuse apologies with accountability.
- Wait on promises that never come.

We are not settling anymore.

We are not begging anymore.

We are not silencing ourselves anymore.

From this moment on, we choose peace over potential.

We choose truth over confusion.

We choose ourselves over half-love.

And when the right love comes?

It won't require begging.

It won't demand you to shrink.

It won't punish you for your needs.

It will see you.

It will choose you.

It will cherish you.

Because the greatest lesson is this:

You were never too much.

She Deserves More Than Potential

You were always enough.

And you always deserved more than potential.

The Standard She Now Walks In

- I do not chase.
- I do not beg.
- I do not explain my worth.
- I do not stay where I am confused.
- I do not settle for potential.

This is not just a book.

This is a transformational experience.

The Crowned Woman Standard Oath

I no longer negotiate with potential.

I evaluate proof.

I no longer romanticize inconsistency.
I require alignment.

I no longer abandon myself to be chosen.
I choose myself first.

I understand now:
Confusion was never chemistry.
Anxiety was never passion.
Intensity was never intimacy.

I was not "too much."
I was under-protected.

That ends now.

From this moment forward:
I measure love by safety.
I measure attraction by peace.
I measure partnership by consistency.

If it costs me my nervous system, it costs too much.

If it requires me to shrink, it is disqualified.
If it asks me to lower my standards, it is not qualified for access.

I do not chase clarity. I demand it.
I do not beg for effort. I expect it.
I do not call red flags "potential." I call them exit signs.

I am no longer available for almost.
I am no longer loyal to possibility.
I am no longer attached to who someone could become.

I honor who they consistently show themselves to be.

And I honor myself enough to walk away.

Proof is my standard.
Ownership is my power.
Peace is my requirement.

I am crowned in discernment.
Grounded in self-respect.
Protected by clarity.

And I will never again abandon myself
for potential.

Signature: ________________________ Date: _______

Other Books by Ernsie Fidelia

When Love Isn't Free: A Story of Love Lost and Strength Found (2025)

No More Silence: Poems of Heartbreak, Healing, and Finding My Voice (2025)

Deserve More Than Potential Workbook: The P.O.P. Method™ Workbook - Proof. Ownership. Peace (2026)

About the Author

Ernsie Fidelia is a bold truth-teller, poet, and spiritual voice for healing. She writes from the raw, unfiltered place between heartbreak and healing. Her words have been called "a mirror, a wound, and a remedy all at once."

Her work speaks to survivors, soul-searchers, and women reclaiming their power after heartbreak and hardship.

Known for her raw honesty and emotional depth, Ernsie writes from lived experience—transforming pain into poetry and silence into strength. She uses poetry and spoken word to reclaim her voice and to speak for women who are still searching for theirs.

Her work reflects her battles with loss, betrayal, love, and the long road back to self-worth.

With *She Deserves More Than Potential*, she shares lessons learned from her own journey of discovering and reclaiming herself.

Through her experience she will teach you how to stand unapologetically in your truth.

This book, like her others, is a blueprint for discovering the patterns that have held you back and provide guidance to help you set your boundaries for what you truly deserve.

Connect with her on Instagram: @AuthorEFidelia

www.ingramcontent.com/pod-product-compliance
Lightning Source LLC
LaVergne TN
LVHW090607110826
845146LV00001B/298

9798999841285